THOUGHTS

FOR DEVELOPING WORLD LEADERS
.................AND PEOPLE...................

Advanced Economies
In Transition
Less Developed
Least Developed

Ben Igiebor

Thoughts for Developing World ....Leaders and People..........

No great improvements in the lot of mankind are possible until a great change takes place in the fundamental constitution of their modes of thought.

John Stuart Mill (1806 – 1873)

DEDICATION

This book is dedicated to my father, Pa Edward Igiebor Obazee, who, sadly, departed this world in the Year of our Lord 1963 but who before leaving, laid the foundation for my education, so, making possible, the writing of this book.

Introduction

Many developing countries are today going through a vicious cycle of mal-administration, bringing upon their citizens poverty, impoverishment, disease, famine, lack of basic amenities, insecurity, homelessness, frustration and lethargy. Many of these countries have become independent of their colonial masters for nearly or over half a century now but they do not appear to have made any progress in the delivery of good governance to their people. In many of them, things have actually degenerated to such a level now that famine threatens millions of their people, unemployment is rampant and economic migration to greener pastures has become the order of the day.

It is the belief of the writer that the situation can still be arrested and things turned around if the leaders will just become accountable to their people, live exemplary lives and very genuinely tackle the problems that beset their countries; the problems are surmountable. In addition, they need to create an atmosphere of security in which economic development, education and research can become entrenched.

In Chapter 1, 'Enough of Music and Dancing', developing world people are called upon to begin to seek solutions to the problems faced by their countries and let go of unproductive pursuits. They are asked to do away with the dependence culture and begin, as the Japanese and Koreans did, not too long ago, to look at some machines or products in common use, make prototypes and to go on improving upon them until they become internationally acceptable.

In Chapter 2, 'Making the best of being Debt-free', many developing countries which benefited from the cancellation of billions of dollars of IMF debts are asked to put their houses in order, make the best of being debt-free, invest their resources in things that will benefit their people and generally improve their lot. The debt-free situation should also act as a great impetus to production, improving their trade and building up their reserves, which in turn will enable them buy more from Europe/North America/Asia thereby contributing to the economies of these regions, which have had their own economic downturns.

'Discriminatory Rates, Freight and Fares' is the title of Chapter 3, in which the financial losses [to developing countries] arising out of the practices of higher charges for their people is highlighted. Suggestions are put forward which, if implemented, will not only end the practices but boost their economies.

In Chapter 4, 'Freedom of Movement' or rather, removal of barriers of entry in international travel is advocated on the grounds that it will foster greater co-operation between people. It also highlights the fact that many developing world migrants in Europe/North America who are 'holed up' because of visa extension/stay permit problems [sometimes for as long as 20 years!] would perhaps not stay as long as they are forced to, if the barriers are removed.

Chapter 5, 'Time to give back stolen booty' is a reproduction of an article in the 'Voice' (a London weekly) which dwelt on goods and gold belonging to Jews confiscated by the Nazis and works of art stolen by the colonial forces from different parts of the world, mainly in develop-ping and third world countries. In follow-up comments, the issue of money embezzled by third world leaders and the undignified role of countries like Switzerland as a haven for these booties are looked at and ideas are put forward on how the artefacts can be returned to their ancestral homes or paid for. The Atlantic slave trade also gets a mention.

Chapter 6 looks at 'The problem of Leadership', highlight-ting those things which developing and third world leaders need to be doing to be seen to be performing well. It then lists certain conditions that all their aspiring leaders should agree, or be made to agree, and to abide by, before their appointment – all in a bid to stamp out corruption, which is the canker-worm devouring their countries' economies.

In Chapter 7, 'Gathering Stubble', the abject conditions under which many developing and third world people li-ving in developed countries have to work is considered; it is very certain that were it not for mal-administration in their home countries, many of the immigrant workers would not be in these countries in the first place, talk less of doing subservient work. The blame is put on their leaders back in their home countries, who are asked to do something about it.

Chapter 8, 'What role Education?' takes a critical look at what the educational institutions have contributed to development of third world countries, whether the investments by their governments in universities that churn out annually hundreds of graduates who do not utilize their knowledge or skills is really worth it and how a bold shift to scientific and industrial research can uplift the countries.

In Chapter 9, Food Sufficiency, the wisdom in importing food that can otherwise grow in third world countries is queried, the possibility of acquisition of large tracks of land for farming in these countries, construction of farmhouses in them and employment of the hundreds of thousands of unemployed youths in town centres in these countries are considered, the aim, to become self-sufficient and less dependent on food importation from far-flung lands.

Chapter 10, 'The Clarion Call' is a call on third world people and leaders to wake up to the fact that they are very, very far behind in the scheme of things, have a lot of catching-up to do, will never be taken seriously until they are seen to be making contributions to human development, instead of being just consumers.

There is a near-total absence of statistics in the work as these appear un-necessary. Besides, the idea is more to get readers go through the book in as short a time as possible and to awaken developing and third world people from their 'deep slumber' in as few pages as possible.

ABOUT THE AUTHOR

The author's first book, African Plants and Trees in Poetry, [a collection of 15 poems and pictures] was written in two weeks in New Cross, Southeast London and published by Amazon.com and its affiliate company, Create Space, in 2013, in Charleston, South Carolina, United States.

He is very widely travelled, having visited the United States, Germany, Holland, Belgium, France and Denmark, then Israel, Turkey, Ivory Coast, Ghana, Tanzania and the Comoros Islands.

He currently resides in Hertfordshire, in the London suburbs.

Ben Igiebor comes from a shipping and maritime background, having trained in shipping management in the offices of the East Asiatic Company in Copenhagen, Denmark [Sept 76 – Dec 77], then Escombe McGrath,

Liverpool and London [Jan – Sept 78] after which he studied International Trade at the London School of Foreign Trade. Thereafter he spent 6 months on sea training on various ships on the Europe/West Africa route, then worked at Alraine Nig. Ltd, Apapa Lagos as Container Operations Manager [1981-85] after which he returned to the UK for an MSc at the University of Wales, Cardiff. He also obtained professional qualifications of both the London Chamber of Commerce and Industry and the Institute of Chartered Shipbrokers. He taught shipping on the professional course at the London Guildhall University – now part of the London Metropolitan University[1990-94].

He is a British citizen, of Nigerian parentage, with three adult children. He is keenly interested in international and current affairs, politics, religion, sports, reading and writing. His first book, African Plants and Trees in Poetry, was published by Amazon/Create Space in the US in 2013 and is available online on Kindle/Amazon and in print. Other books by him are in the pipeline.

He has been recently accepted, to start attending sittings of the All Party Parliamentary Group in Westminster , London, at which African issues are discussed.

CHAPTER ONE

ENOUGH OF MUSIC AND DANCING

According to Christian doctrine, God created man in His own image and likeness and then instructed man to,

> '….increase and multiply and
> fill the earth and subdue it'

Taken literally this means that God wanted man to procreate and populate the earth, which at the time of creation, was just void. He wanted man to be master of all that was upon the earth. He could well have created a million men and women in one go and dispersed them over the earth but then he must have felt that it would be more exciting to see the man that He created reproduce and bring up a new breed of homo-sapiens. He would derive immense joy from seeing man (His creation) do this and exercising the free will that He gave him and for him to take decisions in the process. However, he gave him instructions and the interesting bit was that He wanted to find out if man would obey His bidding.

The other part of the instruction that God gave man was

> 'to subdue the earth'.

By this God meant that man was to develop and exercise con-trol and dominion over every obstacle that there was on earth – these included distance, heights and depths, ocean waves, bad weather, wild animals, lack of shelter and habitation, hunger, disease, etc. God very much wanted to see man bring into play the ingenuity that He imbibed him with, while he struggled against these obstacles. It would give Him great excitement that man, created by Him in His own image, was able to go about these things entirely rely-ing on his intellect, just as a parent likes to see his or her child perform feats. What joy it brings to the parents when their children excel and sadness when they do not.

The idea it seems was that those who excelled in one area would turn out to be successful in other areas, based on the injunction,

> ' To those who have,
> will more be given…'

This is already being manifested in the world today. Indus-trialized countries have benefited a million-fold from their inventions and this has been reflected in the level of deve-lopment and quality of life in their countries. On the con-trary, countries that have not made any effort in the area of inventions are not only losing out in the great game of nations but are now having to sit by and watch their best brains and talents being snatched up and taken away by the team managers in the industrialized countries.

We also see in the bible how man tried to reach the skies by erecting the Tower of Babel, which feat, in those days, equates with the space programmes of modern times. We are told that after the attempt, God felt that if left to his wiles, there was very little that puny man would not be able to accomplish, working together and using the talents He had given him. He therefore caused a division among men in their spoken language and from then on, they could no longer understand one another. As a result, the lofty project had to be abandoned and the people went their different ways. Perhaps this was the beginning of the separation of peoples. Obviously with time and due to economic and political upheavals different groups of people then moved to settle, away from other groups. Gradually the 'uttermost' parts of the earth including the Mediterranean, Africa, Asia and Europe came to be inhabited. From the old world and these areas there were further moves which in time has resulted in the habitable areas of the world being populated.

From the above, we can therefore conclude that the earth has indeed been filled by groups of people made up of different races; for this reason therefore one can say that every race and tribe has complied with the first of the instructions that man was given – that is, to increase and multiply and fill the earth. It cannot however, be said that the same is true of the second part of the instruction, which was to subdue the earth. We have ample records and evidence of man's achievements to date in this area to show that, only a few groups have been performing. The great achievements in agriculture, industry, construction, transportation, science and technology have been made by people from this group. Whether we like it or not, it is obvious that developing and third world people generally have made little or no contribution to 'subduing the earth'.

Perhaps the only area in which the latter have excelled is in music and dancing; one cannot count these as tangible contributions to man's efforts to 'subdue the earth' or improve his conditions on the face of the earth.

Music, it is said, is the food of the soul. There is no gain-saying the fact that music, good music, can 'mellow' the soul, lift the spirit and put laughter and gaiety in the heart of people but other than these, what else does it do?

Music among developing and third world people has, over a long period, been allotted far too much time in the scheme of things – music and dancing at marriage, at childbirth, at puberty, at achieving man-hood or woman-hood, at planting seasons and at harvesting, during nume-rous festivals, masquerades, naming ceremonies, burials, anniversaries, house-warming and material acquisitions, promotion at work, visits by distinguished persons, etc. The list is endless. The people spare themselves no effort or time in their preparation for these colourful events. No doubt about it, there is a lot of artistry and skills displayed in all of these ceremonies and festivals but what tangible benefits are derived from them? Perhaps another way of putting it is, "how much music is essential for a happy life"?

All work and no play, it is said, makes Jack a dull boy but what happens to Jack if it is all play and no work?

Music and dancing are not listed among the essentials of life but it is surprising how very obsessed people have become with it. Time, which can be better spent in other areas of creativity is devoted to making, playing and or listening to music. So many youths are irresistibly drawn by its allure and promise of fame and wealth. In many developping and third world countries today, there is this very crazy competition among budding music hopefuls to get to the top of the music ladder. Rap and contemporary music blare out from night clubs and social gatherings in town centres. The sight of so many young black performers holding on to microphones and dishing out what they earnestly hope will top the charts has left the music landscape with many frustrated youths, who perhaps should be using their talents in other areas of human endeavour. Many of them, could, if they tried, generate brilliant ideas which will help to address some of the pressing problems in their home countries such as housing, transport, water supply, sanitation, etc. Perhaps they could devise new development schemes for their communities, improving food production, road construction or coming up with new materials for building houses, etc. Certainly, these will benefit their people a lot more than the daily diet of music and dancing being fed to them.

It is not proper or right for just one group of people to do all the researching, inventing and manufacturing while other groups merely sit by and enjoy the benefits of their efforts. Is it not rather disturbing for third world leaders that although their people have contributed very little to research and production, they have had no qualms whatsoever at relying on the efforts of other people who have produced today's airplanes, ships, trains, bridges, factories, skyscrapers, vending machines, computers, motor cars, rockets, jet engines, television, cell-phones and i-pads, etc. Is it not even more annoying that these same people aspire to have the best of everything - motor cars, cell-phones, watches, etc?

Certainly no one particular race or group is less well-endowed intellectually than any other; this is borne out by the fact that today, many third world people have studied, trained, lectured and worked alongside their counterparts from the developed countries and have, in many cases, disproved the ugly myth of racial superiority. They have excelled in many instances; there is a national of Nigeria who was a professor of robotics engineering in a US university and many others in various fields today contributing to the American dream. If this is the case, then wherein lies the fault with the third world?

When one considers therefore that quite a number of Asian, African and Latin American nationals have made far-reaching contributions to research and development in the western economies, the question that naturally comes to mind is, 'if they can do it here, why not in their home countries?' The reason appears to be, very sadly, that the right environment does not exist in these countries. Who is to blame? Without any doubt, the 'leaders' who come into power with absolutely no idea what leadership is about and so go about to 'dispense' their own 'doses' of leadership or governance.

Many developing countries have research centres which are headed by people who are unfit to run them, as they have no idea why such centres exist. They collect fat remunerations and once in a year or two, they come up with an 'invention' which is only a slight modification on a tool or product that has been in use in their community for decades. In spite of this, the government continues to pour in funds, just so that some friends or family member or acquaintance can remain employed.

Governments in developing and third world countries seem unaware of the need for self-sustenance, that is, being economically independent. It is easy enough to argue that by the laws of comparative advantage, they do not have to make their own cars, aircraft or other machines – as long as they can afford to pay for these things and obtain them from some other countries, then it is fine. But the fact is, for many of these countries, it is far from fine. There are a number of reasons for this. To be dependent is to have no bargaining power; many third world countries today have no say whatsoever in arriving at the price of produce which they sell to buyers in the developed world – the latter [buyers] dictate the price. Again when it comes to manufactured goods that they buy and import from the developed countries, they also have no say whatsoever on pricing; they pay whatever they are asked to pay and in many cases they are unaware if the goods are over-priced! This places them at a great disadvantage, resulting in their having to pay a lot more for the products and services which they obtain from the developed countries while at the same time obtaining less for what they sell to them. It is a very unfair trading position to be in. One does not need to be a mathematician or economist to know that in such a setting, what follows in the short to long term is economic stagnation. This is particularly true of third world countries where there is over-dependence on primary produce for income generation.

The sum total of the above is that the dependence culture of third world countries on the achievements and inventtions of people of the developed world and their refusal, failure or inability to start making their own products will, in the long run, prove to be their undoing. Unless their leaders realise this and begin to do something to arrest the situation. It is terrible enough as it is at the moment.

What can developing and third world governments do in their various countries to give their people economic independence? Firstly, they need to 'wean' them away from the culture to depend on others while, paradoxically, at the same time wanting the best of everything – from clothing to motor cars! It is incomprehensible that in many developlopping and third world countries where a large part of the population live in abject poverty that quite a number of people like to drive around in Rolls Royce and Jaguar cars, wearing Gucci suits and Rolex watches, which are imported, at great cost and a major drain on foreign exchange. For them, it is alright, so long as it marks them out, from the ordinary people.

There was a story many years ago, of a state governor in Nigeria who was sent a Peugeot 504 car to convey him to a state function and who expressed his anger at being sent such a low-class vehicle to convey him, a governor! One can contrast this with the billionaire owner of Ikea, Sweden who drives comfortably around in a £1,200 Volvo 240 and even sometimes takes public buses! It is qute annoying, when one considers that in the country in question in which the governor refused a Peugeot car, none of the nationals have been able to come up with the technology to make a bicycle, or for that matter, a spanner! It makes a lot of sense that people who have not made meaningful contribution to human development do not get too choosey when it comes to goods and products beyond their ability to manufacture or produce.

One example that clearly illustrates the danger of dependence culture is war planes. Let us say that Country A in a third world country buys all its military hardware from Country B which is developed. War breaks out between them for one reason or the other. It may well be that B had supplied all A's war planes for decades and trained all its pilots. What would then follow is that the supply would automatically end. If A does not have the funding to switch her purchases of war planes to another country or cannot afford the time and expense to train its forces to operate war planes from C, another supplier, then in no time its stock of war planes will become depleted and it will become a question of time before it loses such a war. From the above example one can draw the conclusion that it is unsafe for A to be dependent on B.

War planes have only been used above as an example; this is not to advocate the proliferation of production of weapons of war as this makes the world unsafe. The message for the developing world leaders is that, when the chips are down, every country is better off making its own essential products such as motor cars, trains, planes, computers, machines, etc. While it is financially difficult for the countries to make these items themselves, they can at least do it collectively and begin with the trial production of some simple machines, and improve from there.

Another thing that governments in developing and third world countries need to do to make their people less dependent is to create the right atmosphere for research and also to finance worth-while research projects as well as give encouragement and financial support to the few young people who come up every now and then with one new product or idea. It is indeed sad that very many budding scientists and inventors that have dared to demonstrate their talents in these countries have been consigned to oblivion and not been given any recognition . The following illustrates this;

Prototype of an excavator designed by an ingenious individual in Abuja in Nigeria, but accorded no recognition.

What has often followed is that quite a number of these budding inventors have been picked up by educational and industrial institutions in developed countries, provided the necessary support and found their efforts rewarded. One country's loss becomes another country's gain.

Developing and third world countries would have an uphill task if they were to design, develop and manufacture their own motor cars, trains, ships, airplanes, computers, elevators, machines and so on. The good thing is that they do not have to. All they have to do is to take the cue from the *emerged* 'tiger' economies of Asia, many of which were very undeveloped half a century ago but today boast the most modern motor cars, bullet-trains, electronic equipment, computers and mobile phones.

It is a well-known fact that Japan and Korea started off on the path of development not very long ago. Many of the goods for which they are now famous such as motor cars, motor cycles and machines with the brand names of Honda, Suzuki, Mitsubishi, Toyota, Akai, Samsung, Sony, Aiwa and Sanyo initially began as copies of the design and production of these items that already existed in the world markets, supplied by the developed economies. It was not an easy task for the Asians to learn the intricacies of the engines in these products but that did not deter them. They made proto-type after proto-type, tested them, returned to their drawing boards, re-modelled and re-designed them, reproduced them, tested them and put them into use. Though very unenthusiastic to do so at the beginning due to their low quality, people started to buy these products and use them and before anyone knew it, they had won the buying public over with their 'cheap' brands. The

Japanese and Korean manufacturers did not just stop there; they began to look at ways of improving the products and adding on to them bit and pieces that made them more desirable to buyers.

The efforts of the Japanese, Koreans and Chinese have been complemented by abundant and cheap labour (which is also readily available in the developing and third world) which has made it possible for their manufactured goods to compete very well in the global market for recognition and patronage. The 'tiger' economies have been going from strength to strength for decades now and their products have flooded markets world-wide. The significance for them, which developing and third world leaders and people should well take note of, is that they have now earned the respect and recognition of the erstwhile leaders of the industrialized world. They are now able to stand on their own, are even looked up to, are heard (not just seen) at major international conferences and become important players in the world game.

The good thing in all these is that the Asian 'tiger' economies have set the perfect example for developing and third world countries' leaders and people to emulate. All they have to do is to put to use the abundant human resources at their disposal by

a] challenging and setting targets for their research establish-ments for new ideas and products and

b] engaging the cheap labour available in the production processes.

It is on record that many nationals of India, Sri Lanka, Nigeria, Ghana, Kenya, Brazil, Indonesia, etc have been going over to the industrialized countries for studies and training. Such studies have included courses in engineering, technology, the sciences, architecture, etc. At the same time, many hundreds of thousands of graduates in these fields have been 'churned' out by universities in the countries in question, with many going on to acquire post-graduate and doctoral qualifications from universities abroad.

The question that arises is, having acquired the necessary skills for research work needed for industrial progress, why have developing and third world leaders not encouraged these young people to make meaningful input to the development of their countries? Is there not a need for governments to come up with defined and clear policies aimed at achieving self-reliance and sustenance? Is the problem that they cannot see the advantages?

If we take the example of the common motor car, there is absolutely no reason why countries like Saudi Arabia, Nigeria, Pakistan, Mexico and South Africa, with all the material and human resources at their disposal, have not produced their first indigenous motor cars, after decades of independence. This should have happened many years ago. One is not talking about assembling cars from CKDs [completely-knocked-down components] imported by containers from Europe. Here we are talking about the countries people building their own cars.

To achieve the above, all that is needed is for the government in each country to bring together, in a purpose-built research village, a group of qualified mechanical engineers from some very good engineering institutions and an equal number of very experienced motor mechanics from some excellent motor mechanic workshops in the country. The sole objective will be to come up with a car in 3 to 5 years, at all costs and no matter what it takes. A group leader would be appointed and given clear guidelines, full provision made for all the requirements for the successful execution of the project, with the families of the project members catered for all through the project life. Fairly old models of say 3 – 5 cars should be acquired and given to the team to dismantle, study, analyse, sketch and work on, over many months and then, based on their findings, begin, say in the second or third year, to model and design what they believe will be their first car. If a programme such as this had been embarked upon, say 5 or 10 years ago in any of these countries, there is every likelihood that by now, they would have made a break-through and made their own car by now. Others will follow.

Africa

Ghana's talented but ignored inventors

A father and his pilot son in a country with no history of manufacturing are making products that will stun the world.

[Kent Mensah](#) Last updated: 24 Aug 2014 20:16

Accra, Ghana - Imagine having a television set that comes on after an effortless clap or by blowing air; picture yourself in a car that is engineless and starts with a simple push of a button tucked to your dress; or a change-over-machine that speaks and tells you where exactly a fire or electrical fault is in your home.

This is not fiction. It is not magic. It is not happening in Europe or Asia and not even in the United States. These products are being manufactured in the West African nation of Ghana.

The brains behind this is Apostle Dr Kwadwo Safo, owner of the Kantanka Group of Companies. He is naturally gifted. A genius. An inventor and a philanthropist. He has no formal or sophisticated technical background. He imagines, dreams and creates at will. He lives in his own world.

It takes about 45 minutes from Accra, the capital, to reach his "city" at Gomoa Mpota in the central region of Ghana. It is set apart from the hustle and bustle of cosmopolitan Accra. His flag - blue, red, yellow and white stars embossed on the blue hue - constantly flies at a junction on the highway you reach after going past beautiful green landscapes that lead to his location.

It is a large tract of land. The buildings are huge. The ambiance is engaging. It has a natural touch and feel, complete with tortoises - the oldest is 40 years - and a porcupine, evidence of Safo's love for nature.

Engineless car

A large African map showing a picture of Apostle Safo spinning a ball imprinted with pictures, a huge star beneath it and a miniature aircraft welcome visitors.

It takes close to two-and-a-half hours to tour his complex in a car. His son, Kwadwo Safo Jnr, a commercial pilot who acquired his licence at age 19, welcomed Al Jazeera. He is the group's chief operations officer.

After driving past the tortoises, the first point of call was a workshop where a chopper was being manufactured alongside a hand-made engineless five-seater vehicle.

The whites believed in themselves and got to where they are now. They are no different from us. We all stayed in our mothers' womb for nine months

 - Safo Jnr, Chief Operations Officer of the Kantanka Group of Companies

Safo Jnr said they will ensure there is no risk in test-flying the chopper and explained how the engineless car will work.

"The non-engine vehicle does not rely on a combustion engine to move, but an electric motor powered by rechargeable batteries," Safo Jnr told Al Jazeera.

"The batteries can be recharged with solar energy or electricity. As you drive the car on the road, it converts the energy from the sun into mechanical energy which powers the car.

"We do everything here. For the engineless car it is only the lights and the tyres that were bought. Everything else from moulding [parts], among others, was done by our local people."

A peacock bade us goodbye from that section, then three zebras smiled at us as we drove on an untarred road towards the colossal buildings on the outskirts. They are four in all, neatly painted and look abandoned when viewed from a distance.

The structures serve as the assembling plants for the yet-to-be unveiled Kantanka range of commercial vehicles - sports utility vehicles (SUVs) and pickup trucks.

Although some car parts are imported, assembling the more than 1,500 pieces for a car and spraying are done by about 20 young men between the ages of 16-25 years. Amazingly, they have no formal training in building a car.

"Most of them are junior and senior high school leavers. The people who are actually racking their brains here to make things work have never been to school before," Safo Jnr said.

Six to 10 cars can be assembled and be ready for the road in a day. Four had been completed and tested by the time Al Jazeera visited. It is hard to tell they were actually assembled in Ghana, save for the Kantanka crown and inscription at the back.

Market plans

"We are hoping to increase the number to 12 or 15 daily when we go commercial soon," Safo Jnr said.

"We have delayed ... going commercial because Africans and Ghanaians in general have the perception that once it is from Ghana, it is not good - durability is not assured, safety is not guaranteed. So we have decided to use the products ourselves and make sure they are good to go and standardised before we hit the market.

"I was in Brazil about six months ago and I was in tears. The whole of Rio de Janeiro was packed with Marcopolo buses ... and these are buses that were assembled and made in Brazil.

"They patronise it. In India they encourage made-in-India vehicles - like Mahindra - and that's my dream to one day see Kantanka cars on the streets of Accra, Kumasi and all over. I will be fulfilled," a visibly euphoric Safo Jnr pointed out in his office fitted with a locally made air-conditioner that is switched on and off by slotting in a card.

The card in the air-conditioner, explained Safo Jnr, works like one used for an ATM. It is programmed to start the air-conditioner, regulate the temperature and can tell the time when the unit should be turned off. It is multi-functional, he said.

Difficult questions

While hugely ambitious and a potential source of pride for a country that is only known for its gold, cocoa and lately oil, the Kantanka project still raises major questions. Who, for example, will buy SUVs in a country where the average income is $1,400 and where just about everyone drives a used car? Do the carmakers perform crash tests, and will they meet the high standards of cars made in Europe and Asia?

"We will be doing that in the course of our manufacturing process," said Safo Jnr, referring to crash tests.

The cars will be "affordable" and middle-income earners will be able to buy them. "We know the market and we can assure you that Africans will be able to buy our cars," he said.

In some countries projects such as this attract financial assistance from the government. But Ghanaian governments upon governments seem to have ignored the "Star of Africa", as Apostle Dr Safo is called by the people of Ghana.

Not even his self-made Limousine dubbed "Obrempong", the speaking change-over-machine, or a range of flat-screen television sets made with wood covers that respond to a simple clap to come alive, increase or reduce volumes have fascinated the government enough to support one of their own.

Determined to succeed

The Safo family is undaunted though.

"Most of the promises they have made, they say they are in the pipelines. I'm sure African pipelines are very choked so the water is not flowing. Not even the corporate world has shown concern … We are still hoping," said Safo.

"We have had several offers from Asia and Europe, but we turn them down because we just want to stay in Africa and make sure that whatever we are doing here we'll be able to achieve our dreams.

"People tell us that we are wasting our time because we won't get anywhere. But we pay no attention to them, rather we make sure that we prove them wrong by meeting targets that we set for ourselves."

The US-trained young pilot is optimistic about the future. For him, it is a matter of trust and belief in the African.

"The whites believed in themselves and got to where they are now. They are no different from us. We all stayed in our mothers' womb for nine months ... If you cut a white and a black man you get blood. The only differences are our names and colours," he said.

"So we should believe in ourselves. We must reduce the talking and put in work."
Source:
Al Jazeera

There are obvious advantages to developing and third world countries to start making their own motor vehicles, affordable to the citizenry. Firstly, the amount of foreign exchange used for vehicle import will be drastically reduced, with the savings going into other areas of development. For a country the population of say, Egypt or Nigeria, this may be hundreds of millions of pounds or dollars, which otherwise will be pumped into the already buoyant economies of developed countries. This is the aspect that should interest developing and third world leaders; invest now in projects for vehicle production either individually or collectively on a regional basis and save your treasuries a great deal of money, create jobs and do away with the dependence culture. Do nothing and continue to waste foreign exchange and create jobs in countries which they import cars from. This is the stark situation.

Apart from creating employment locally, embarking on car production will position any country on its way to establishing its industrial base. From this, progress will be made towards the construction of other machines, boats and ferries, locomotives, motor-cycles, etc. Agreeably not every developing or third world country has the resources to do these things on their own but there are a number of them that can, if they put their effort and resource into it.

The message for developing and third world leaders is that they have to wake up and start doing something to put things on the right track in their countries. Otherwise, they will be left out of reckoning in the scheme of things. The very care-free attitude towards creativity, invention, breaking new grounds etc must be erased from the culture of developing and third world people and in its place the leaders must find ways to inculcate in the minds of their people inquiring minds, challenging thoughts and the desire to improve the conditions in which they find themselves.

It might be pertinent, at this point, with regards to the above, to look at the views of one Peregrine Worsthorne [who was a lead writer for the New Statesman] on race, racism and how they re-late to human development.

.

Thought control is not the answer

Peregrine Worsthorne examines the roots of his generation's racist beliefs

BY PEREGRINE WORSTHORNE PUBLISHED 5 MARCH, 1999 - 12:00

TWEET WIDGET

Like so many Britons of my generation, I am both racist and anti-racist, the former prejudice feeding, indeed causing, the latter. It is because I am so aware of my racism that I feel obliged to be fiercely anti-racist. My racism is kept well under control by my anti-racism; more than under control, positively overwhelmed, as much in my private thoughts as in public utterances.

How did my racism develop in the first place? Let me explain what race relations were in the recent past. In the interwar years, when I was growing up, it was in the air one breathed. Darwin had taught us that survival was the well-earned privilege of the fittest. In the heyday of European imperialism and with the map painted mostly red, the white Anglo-Saxon race, judged by Darwin's test, was the fittest of all.

The better-educated among us were aware that the brown and yellow races had enjoyed glorious civilisations in the past. But manifestly they had all fallen by the wayside, to be overtaken by the whites. As for the blacks, they had - as far as we could see - never been in the running: no literature, little art, no political institutions worthy of the name, past or present.

Accordingly, it was the duty of the whites to take charge of human progress; and if this required white domination of the lesser breeds - even their extinction in the case of the Maoris, the Aboriginals and Red Indians - then so be it. Even Trollope, that most genial of liberal Victorian novelists, was quite explicit on this point. At the end of a travel book about Australia he concluded that it was probably a kindness to let the Aboriginals drink themselves to death since they could have no acceptable future in the modern world.

In short, we were taught that racism and progress went hand in hand. Eventually the non-white races, under white tuition, would be rendered fit enough to rejoin the great human ascent, but in the meantime there was no responsible way the white races could avoid taking up the burden and soldiering on.

So much for the roots of my racism; as for the roots of my anti-racism, they are more difficult to identify. With the case of anti-Semitism it was the Holocaust; with the browns, probably Nehru and the success of democratic India; and with the yellows, the amazing triumph of the postwar Japanese economy. With the blacks, however, it was more personal and I can pinpoint the moment. About five years ago I wanted to put up a second-generation black immigrant friend for a London club.

Previously the only black men I had known were servants in southern Africa or would-be revolutionaries, with none of whom had there been any personal relationship remotely powerful enough to affect my assumptions of white racial superiority. But with this black friend it was different and the thought that his candidature for the club in question was being questioned because of the colour of his skin set me furiously to think. Laughable you will say, but there it is.

Another incident followed. I watched a London taxi driver reject an eminently respectable-looking black lawyer in favour of a group of white soccer louts. More grist to my anti-racist mill came from spending a richly entertaining month making a television programme about race with that quintessential Englishman - cricketer, *NS* columnist and Shakespeare fan - Darcus Howe, in which he came out as much more optimistic about the state of race relations in this country than I did. Finally, there was Nelson Mandela.

I confess to these somewhat insubstantial anti-racist roots only to make the point that if I, an Oxbridge undergraduate etc, was so deeply affected by the racist assumptions of the 19th and 20th centuries, and has only come to abandon them by a series of experiences more to do with class than race, then some measure of toleration is owed to less fortunate white citizens, from lower down the educational ladder, whose inherited and deeply ingrained racial prejudices, instead of being mitigated through friendships with black immigrants - as mine were - have been exacerbated through competition with them for jobs and houses.

Which brings me to the problem of racism in the police force. According to the Macpherson report into the Stephen Lawrence case, the police tend to treat black citizens with notably less sensitivity than they treat white citizens. But until about 25 years ago this was how the police treated working-class citizens - that is, with notably less sensitivity than they treated middle- or upper-class citizens. There must be many working-class families who remember getting the same kind of treatment as that meted out to the Lawrence family. One law for the rich; one for the poor.

But nobody then recommended new thought-control laws to change these attitudes. The very idea would have chilled the blood. But as classes became increasingly indistinguishable, attitudes did change and in my view, as more and more blacks become recognisably middle class, so attitudes to them will change as well, as they are already beginning to do. Believe it or not, a few days ago I saw a white London taxi driver reject a white lawyer fare for a black one, and another black friend has just been elected to the Beefsteak club.

Extreme situations, like a murder inquiry, will be the last to experience these changes. Under that kind of intense strain, the police will go on stereotyping blacks as criminals and blacks will go on stereotyping the police as pigs. But these situations are not representative and it is madness, in a hysterical response to the Lawrence case, to react as if they were. Yet this is what the government is doing. Serious consideration is being given to the introduction of new laws to prohibit not only racist actions but also racist thoughts, on the grounds that such unprecedentedly repressive measures are needed to drive out what Macpherson calls institutional racism.

Nothing could be more certain, in my view, to put back the clock with a vengeance, and I can already feel the dying embers of my own racism beginning to flare up again.

For if racism is bad, attempts at thought control would be far, far worse and were it now officially accepted that the only way to realise the ideal of a multiracial Britain would be to install Big Brother, then I, for one, would be sorely tempted to return to the roots out of which, in every sense, my racism grew.

CHAPTER TWO

MAKING THE BEST OF A DEBT-FREE SITUATION

Over a decade ago many developing and third world countries and economies were groaning severely under very harsh and extremely difficult conditions brought about by external debts. No doubt about it, the conditions were self-inflicted, as no one country was compelled to go out and apply for loans. It was a time when the World Bank was awash with petrol-dollars and development projects in third world countries were crying for funding. So third world leaders took advantage of the situation and went, bowl-in-hand, to the agency set up to dispense the loans, the International Monetary Fund. A large number of the leaders secured loans on terms and conditions that were unfavourable to them but either did not know or did not care and went ahead. The rate of interest applied on these loans were prohibitive and operated on the basis of compound interest, meaning that over time, interest began to accrue on both capital and interest, to the detriment of many of the countries. In no time, two hundred and fifty million dollar loans became billion dollar debts and kept growing, at an astronomical rate.

According to Joseph Hanlon and Ann Pettifor [in a research carried out in 2000] the debt habit was a cycle of lenders 'pushing' loans on borrowers and then turning a blind eye to their misuse and....adding more conditions to new lending to offset the initial loans.

The questions to answer are many. Why did many developping and third world countries fall into the trap and accept the loans? How much of the loans went into development projects? How many such projects have turned out to be good investments for every country that took the loans? With the signatories to these loans now out of power in many of these countries, who takes responsibility for the negative effects the loans have had on the economies?

The debts owed to the World Bank rose astronomically from $54billion in 1964 to $2,500billion in 2000. For the 60 low-income countries that took the loan, their share amounted to $532billion, with African countries alone owing $300billion. The debts were insidious, affecting all aspects of economic and social life and perpetuating poverty, with governments in most African countries spending more on debt-repayment than on health care or education. The projects for which loans were advanced all had strong economic commercial bias and paid no attention to poverty reduction, resulting in increased debt burdens in countries such as Philippines, Brazil, Rwanda and Ghana. From 1980 to 1996 sub-Saharan African nations paid back as interest, double the sum total of the original loans they took, plus there was thrice more for them to pay!

However due to the outcry worldwide against the continued injustice of the debts, efforts began for addressing the problem. In March 1999, Canada decided it would act to respond to the needs of severely indebted countries. In September the same year, US President Clinton stated that the US would try and forgive all the debt poor countries owed to the US if they would use the money saved on health, education and other basic human needs. In December, the UK promised to cancel all of the debt owed by 26 poor countries if the savings could be put to poverty eradication. Following all the above, Germany followed suit and promised action to write off a huge slice of the debts it was owed by poor countries.

ECGD Debt Relief for African Countries - 2006/07

Country £(thousands)	ECGD Debt
Cameroon	25,870
Cote d'Ivoire	240
Ghana	6,900
Guinea	10
Malawi	232
Nigeria	1,648,916
Sierra Leone	60
Togo	30
Zambia	1,160

Source : Statistics on International Development 2002-2007

In May 2001 international communities came together and agreed to seek a moratorium on debt service payments for the world's most indebted countries, particularly those in exceptional circumstances such as civil wars, famine, floods or other natural disasters. All these were followed by protests worldwide the main one being the Jubilee 2000 event held in London and a number of G8 summits.

As at today, international loans worth more than $90billion have been cancelled for 34 countries which have agreed to introduce poverty-reduction schemes in them – these include Benin, Burkina Faso, Burundi, Cameroon, Ghana, Liberia, Madagascar, Malawi, Mali, Mauritania, Niger, Rwanda, Senegal, Uganda and Zambia in Africa. It is note-worthy that Uganda is one country that has put its savings from debt cancellation to good use – it all went into a Po-verty Action Fund and was used for building new school classrooms, resulting in a rise in school attendance from 2.5million to 7million in 4 years, after debt-reduction in 1997. Also in Tanzania, the savings was used to eliminate school fees and Burkina Faso used its savings to drastically reduce the cost of life-saving drugs and increase access to clean water.

Now that the developed nations have taken the proactive approach and written off most of the debts owed by the world's poorest nations, what lies ahead for these coun-tries? This is the question that their leaders need to be addressing, at this point in time.

The decision by many developing and third world coun-tries to take the IMF loans was not a popular one among the people; it sparked off debates and protests in many of the countries – the proponents spelling out the advantages and the opponents high-lighting the dangers. Many leading and distinguished economists who could see the 'strings' in the offers clamoured for their rejection. In leading national daily newspapers, on television and radio and at rallies there was an outcry against their acceptance. Despite all the hue and cry however, many third world leaders went on and took the loans, lured like hungry fishes to their baits. Did they know what they were doing? Were they aware that their action would create untold hardships for their nationals and generations yet unborn? Did they believe the loans could easily be repaid, really?

In almost every case the leaders knew quite well that it was not in the best interest of their countries to take the loans. They were driven by selfish desires and greed. The loans presented them wonderful opportunities to enrich themselves through grandiose projects with loopholes for siphonning funds to private bank accounts in foreign lands. It did not matter to them if the projects failed or the portion of the loans invested was lost or worst of all, their countries saddled with massive debts that could never be repaid. They reckoned that they would not have to take personal responsibility for the repayment of the debts anyway and in any case, they would quit government before the hardships set in. All that mattered to them was to get a slice of it and save it in foreign vaults – and with the proceeds be able to acquire mansions in different cities and locations in the world, fly first-class for the rest of their lives, send their children to the best private schools in the world, keep mistresses and live life to the fullest, while most of their countrymen and women would be wallowing in abject poverty. These were people without any conscience whatsoever, intent on satisfying their selfish desires at the expense of millions of innocent people who are then made to suffer for their actions. As far as they were concerned, they were laying up treasures for their off-springs but what is the guarantee that they [the off-springs] would get to enjoy them?

The sad thing is that most of the so-called leaders who took and mismanaged the loans are very much alive and kicking today, in palatial settings in their countries and in positions where they not only influence authority but are able to lay hands on more of the wealth of their countries. It should be quite possible today to draw up a list of the people who took the loans in every country that took them; it would be an interesting subject for research, the findings of which will shock many decent people. Perhaps a body such as the United Nations should sponsor and fund such work with a view to compiling a global list of mal-administrators who contributed to the malaise in their home countries today. Perhaps when such a list is circu-lated, it will discourage those whose names appear on it from continuing to flaunt their ill-gotten wealth and learn the hard truth that at the end of the day, crime does not pay. It will also act as a deterrent to current leaders.

Despite the heavy burden brought to bear on the citizenry such as currency devaluation, removal of all forms of sub-sidy, increase in transport costs, higher tax and value-added tax, etc, there are very few countries where the loan was taken that have seen any progress whatsoever. Ghana is an example of a country where IMF policies have worked but it is actually an overstatement. More than anything else, Ghana has benefited greatly from the mass exodus of people who fled the country in its moment of economic stagnation and who found their ways to 'greener pastures' in the developed countries and started to send home remittances, which to a very large degree, helped to lift up the economy from its dire straits; to complement this was the

fact that the country's leader Retired Gen. Rawlings had sent a chilling message to everyone that corruption in high places would not be tolerated. If these two factors were absent it is uncertain that Ghana would have been able to get back to where it is today. From Asia to Africa and on to South America it is difficult to pinpoint one developing and third world country that took the loan and utilized it for any worth-while project from which its citizens are benefiting. Hospitals without drugs, water pipes in homes with no water, rubbish dumps in city centres, rickety buses used for mass transport in urban areas, intermit-tent power supply, poorly equipped universities, etc in these parts of the world suggest very clearly that IMF loans were any-thing but helpful to the economies of these countries.

However, since many of the bad debts of the third-world countries have been written off, the economies of many of these countries have been growing steadily and particularly so in Africa. Growth rates of 7% and above have been recorded for many of the countries. This has been possible, in part, due to the tighter rules by which the economies of these nations, tied to the apron strings of world financial institutions, have been opera-ting. The economies have also experienced massive upsurge in investments particularly from China, which have helped to build new railway systems and roads that have helped to boost the movement of goods.

Considering that these growth figures have only begun to be recorded only after writing off the debts, it is correct to con-clude that developing and third world countries have become the better for it. For now at least, their leaders and people can look with greater optimism at the future and expect greater improvement in the lifestyles they would lead.

A note of warning need to be sounded at this point for the benefit of third world people. In those countries where oil has become the mainstay of their economies among these people, the leaders must guard against embarking on white elephant projects that will not impact positively on the lives of the people. For example, investing in space travel as was recently rumoured to be on the cards for the go-vernment of Nigeria or building nuclear power stations that are prohibitively expensive to set up and maintain, not to mention the inherent dangers they pose, should be discouraged in many of these countries. Most, if not every third world country, have abundant sources of renew-able energy sources and so do not have to go nuclear. Rather, they need to create the enabling environment for their crops of young graduates in the science disciplines to come up with new ideas and products that can contribute to world progress. As earlier stated, this is the only sure and certain way to bring developing countries and third world people to the level at which they can operate as equals with people of developed countries.

In conclusion, third world countries that have benefited from debt-cancellation are asked to put their economies in order, make the best of being debt-free, invest their resources in projects that will benefit their people and generally improve their lot. The debt-free situation should become a great impetus to research, scientific endeavours, production and manufacturing, improving trade and building up their foreign reserves which in turn will help them buy more from the developed nations which are currently experiencing economic hardship.

CHAPTER THREE

DISCRIMINATORY RATES AND FARES

In the last year or so, there has been a clamour in Nigeria against discriminatory flight fares quoted and applied to Nigerian air travellers by the major European airlines. Surprisingly though, when one would have expected the complaint to be about the higher rates on routes to Africa by these airlines vis-à-vis fares to the Americas and Australia and Hong Kong, the Nigerians are unhappy that they are charged a higher fare than travellers to Ghana! This should not at all be the bone of contention.

A careful look at a newspaper or online general quotation by major European and American airlines always show that fares to most African destinations are in the main, usually 25 to 60 higher than what are charged to destinations of equal distances in the Americas, Australia and Hong Kong. This is clearly an unfair and discriminatory practice and not in the best interest of the Africans. For some reasons however, it is unknown that any African leader has ever taken up the issue with the airlines concerned. While it may well be considered rather unimportant, it is pertinent to point out to third world leaders that their nationals are losing a great deal of foreign exchange while purchasing their travel tickets. A simple calculation will throw light on this.

Let us assume for example that 400,000 Ghanaians travel by air every year from Accra to the UK. Currently, the ticket fare would be something in the region of £850. Considering that a return ticket from say, New York, USA which is equidistant, costs £350, one would naturally want to ask why it would not be the same amount on the Accra to UK ticket - £500, being the difference is a great deal of money! Taking into consideration that about 400,000 travel per year, we are talking of an annual excess payment of the sum of £200,000,000.00! From this point, it is easy to see how much is being unnecessarily lost by the Ghanaian economy. Over a 5-year period, we are talking of £1 billion! Such an amount no doubt, will go a long way towards the construction of several local hospitals or educational institutions or the provision of affordable housing for hundreds of thousands of its citizens. Loss on a such a colossal scale running into hundreds of millions annually is unjustifiable and raises two questions;

a] what is the justification for this disparity?

b] why has it been allowed to go on unchecked?

c] considering that developing and third world countries are considered the poorer members of the global community why do they have to bear the burden of higher travel costs?

d] finally, are third world leaders unaware of this injustice?

e] if so, what are they doing about it?

It appears that the only reason why developing countries and third world governments and leaders have never bothered about these malpractices in commerce and travel is the fact that those at the very top are unaffected by whatever is charged their people. For one thing, they can easily afford to pay for these services, either from their own pockets or from the coffers of government. This is gross irresponsibility and negation of duties to their citizenry, whose interests they swore to uphold at the inception of their administration. The action results in the loss of hundreds of millions of dollars annually by many of these cash-starved countries.

Also, because individuals bear the brunt of these malpractices, no one really ever bothers to raise the issue at any gathering. They do however need the 'protection' of their governments, which are there, not merely to protect their borders and prevent military incursions but also to look after their personal interests. The area of freight rates, travel fares and charges is one in which unwary citizens of third world countries are currently being made to pay, albeit very dearly, for services and goods that they require and for which citizens in the developed world pay much less.

One other issue that needs to be high-lighted is surcharges that many unwary developing countries and third world people are made to pay every time they ship goods from Europe to their countries. Taking a container of goods again as an example, every shipper would normally have to pay the standard freight rate, which may or may not be fair. In addition however, for most shipments by sea to developlopping and third world countries, the shippers are lumbered with additional charges which do not exist in trades between the developed countries. The so-called surcharges are levied merely on the assumption that something is likely to happen which will add to the cost [for the shipping line] of actually moving the consignment from say Europe to Africa or Bangladesh. The likely events are listed as currency devaluation, a rise in fuel prices, congestion in ports, labour disputes or strikes, etc. The assumption – in the case of currency surcharge, for example – is that, where after collection of freight on a consignment to a specific destination that the value of the local currency falls, the shipping line would need to make good any loss it would suffer as a result of such devaluation. However, where no such devaluation takes place, no refunds are made to the unwary shipper!

Also because oil prices might rise and shipping lines might have to purchase fuel [or bunkers as is known in shipping] at a higher rate for their vessels in the course of the voyage they levy a small percent of the standard freight rate as fuel surcharge, which again is never refunded, if the situation did not arise. A surchar-ge for war or congestion or some other likely event may be added [usually compounded] and at the end of the day, the ship- per is made to pay something in the region of an additional 25 percent. All well and good for the ship-owner – the shipper has purchased the goods and has no option but to ship them.

Now, one would expect that where these charges have been collected in advance and none of the expected events happen, that refunds would be made. However the ship-owner does not do the honourable thing and offer refunds but keeps the charges. Invariably, the shipper, having been able to collect his consignment forgets about the surcharge he has had to pay. To quantify this, if we assume that Ghana imports 120,000 TEUS [20-foot equivalent units – of containers] every year from the UK and for each unit the sum of £280 is collected as surcharges, then it follows that £33,000,000.00 is collected as surcharges, which rightly, should be refunded. It is easy enough to make out, who benefits from these charges. Certainly not developing country and third world shippers, for that matter.

As earlier indicated, surcharges such as the above have more or less been long removed from trades between developed coun-tries who know well enough that it is an ignoble way for ship-operators to make undue profit and who know that their people need to be protected against such mal-practices. The problem for many developing countries and third world leaders and governments is that they are either not aware, or are not fully aware of what they are losing to unscrupulous big-time traders as a result of the mal-practices. It does not matter if those who suffer from them directly are the individual shippers; at the end of the day, developing and third world countries are losing colossal amounts of money that they can ill-afford to, what with water, roads, electricity and housing projects begging for such funds. The sad part of it all is that annually, many of the countries in the third world go, cap-in-hand begging for aid [for far smaller amounts than they are losing in the first place] from European countries. Sometimes, the latter make the initial moves in providing 'aid' to these countries, as a way of 'showing concern' for their plight.

On the issue of air fares again, many big operators have put forward the argument [in favour of high fares] to developing countries that the fact that the routes are un-economical necessitates the higher fares. They argue further that on their own, the routes cannot sustain themselves and have to be reimbursed by profits on other routes. This is however a lame argument, as no evidence is ever provided to back it up. It is difficult to believe that an airline that flies two wide-bodied aircraft from Europe to Nigeria or India daily does not make enough profit to sustain business on the routes. If not enough profit is being made, then the logical thing to do would be to pack it in and leave it to others. Or are we to believe that they are doing the nationals of the country a favour. Another rumour making the rounds is that governments and national airlines in many developing and third world countries actually like the fares to be arbitrarily high; if this is so, then it is sad indeed as it shows a gross dereliction of responsibility on the part of the leaders for the welfare of their citizens. Allegations of 'sweeteners' provided these leaders by foreign airlines [to keep the fares high] are difficult to prove but cannot be ruled out.

The message for developing countries and third world leaders is quite clear – they have the interests of their nationals, first and foremost, to protect, before that of the foreign airlines. Most of the leaders swore on oath, on assuming office, to protect their citizens and allowing foreign airlines to exploit them is certainly no way of doing so. In the developed economies, the interest of the people is paramount and something that is jealously guarded and protected. It is a relegation of duty and the oath to which they are sworn, for leaders of developing countries to turn a blind eye to their countrymen and women being ripped off by foreign airlines.

As they say, travelling is a good way of educating people. Most young people and students in Europe and North America can afford and do go on holidays every year, thereby widening their knowledge. But if one may ask, how many young people or university students in Pakistan can afford to travel to say, Sri Lanka or Malaysia on holiday? Or in the same vein, a group of people from Bolivia or Paraguay to Mexico or the US? In fact, how many Indian youngsters or students can afford to go on holiday to Saudi Arabia or Bahrain, which is close by? Neither are Congolese or Angolan youths or students able to raise the funds to go on air travel to say, Cameroun, Uganda or Ghana.

The message is that this is no longer an age in which young people should be allowed to languish in ignorance and poverty simply because it has always been so. Making air travel for developing countries and third world people more affordable should be encouraged as it will go a long way to removing all the barriers such as racial prejudice, ignorance, etc that mar global interaction and international trade.

PRICING OF PRODUCE

It is a well-known fact that for most developing countries, their economies depend to a large extent on primary produce, basically palm produce from Malaysia and West Africa, rice and cotton from Asia, India, Sri-Lanka etc, tea and coffee from South America, Sri Lanka, East Africa, etc. Timber is also a major export produce. Most of these items are cultivated and harvested for their cash values and proceeds from their export constitute for the countries, the only foreign exchange earned. On the basis of what they earn, the countries have to make provision for their imports of food, medicines, machinery, vehicles, industrial plants, aircraft, overseas training, education, etc.

For many of the countries, the gross income from the export of these produce comes to only several hundred million pounds or dollars, which is hardly ever enough to meet their most basic requirements in the areas listed above. It is the belief of this writer that the revenue from these exports can be increased to a large extent if the producing countries can come together and form trading organisations that will act in their interest. Cocoa producing countries will form an umbrella organisation for the purpose and so will those producing tea, coffee, palm oil and produce, cotton, rice, etc. Current international trade practices have been unfavourable, for far too long, to developing countries in that the latter have had virtually no say in the pricing of their primary produce or the end-products; the processing companies in the developed economies dictate what is paid, without input by the producers! This is very unfair and it is one main issue that the type of organisations envisaged above should begin to look into.

Another matter that should also interest such bodies is the control of the quantity of produce exported annually; ceilings need to be set to ensure that there is no over-supply in the market, which the buyers can exploit. For example, if Malaysia, Indonesia, Ghana and Nigeria set up a body of oil-palm producers, just like OPEC for oil, once the total annual demand for the produce by foreign manufacturers of soap and cosmetics can be determined, the countries in question should then agree to produce just about enough every year to meet the demand. They would therefore be allocated quotas and control measures put in place to ensure compliance. The only reason why the foreign buyers of produce have for decades been able to dictate the prices is because the producing countries have been over producing, resulting in a glut, which allows the buyers to take charge and control the pricing mechanism. The producers are forced to accept whatever price they are offered, prices plummet and the cycle continues. It would not be a big surprise if it turns out that buyers of produce in Europe and North America may have, for decades, been underpaying the producers up to the tune of 60%! That should be undoubtedly, an interesting subject for research.

Perhaps developing countries should take matters one step further by demanding that processing and manufacturing of the end-products should henceforth be done in the producing countries. For a start they could begin making half-finished products which would cost a lot less to transport to the processing plants abroad. Apart from ensuring that the producers get more money for every ton of their produce, this would also create employment for a large number of job-seekers. There is no reason why Cadbury cannot process and produce its cocoa-based products near the sources of cocoa and then export the end-products to Europe, America and Asia. The same can be said for coffee. It is however up to the leaders in the developing world to raise the matter; in the long run, the move will boost their their countries' economies and ensure that the bulk of the proceeds from the sale of their crops/produce get to them.

A case from Venezuela:

Over the weekend Nicolas Maduro, socialist president of Venezuela, announced that he was forcing a local chain of electronics stores to sell its products at cheaper prices. Maduro is now seeking the power to extend this policy to other goods, in an attempt to "protect the people from the bourgeois parasites".

The above report, in Nov 2013, clearly illustrates the frustration of the Vene zuelan leader at the sky-high prices, his people were being made to pay, for foreign products, prices they had no input, in arriving at.

CHAPTER FOUR

FREEDOM OF MOVEMENT

Following on the achievements of the United States in the economic arena in the last 200 years and publicity that went with the sales of American products such as Ford cars, Coca Cola refreshment drinks, jeans trousers, emblazoned T-shirts, etc and reports sent back home by earlier immigrant settlers, the idea of going over to the US began in the 50's and 60's to appeal to hundreds of thousands of young people in the developing world. Having scanned their home-fronts, so to say, and finding that these presented very little opportunities for break-through, the urge to travel abroad to the more developed countries began to gain ground among them. In the US, they envisaged the attainment of their ambitions of good jobs, dream homes, cars, etc and living life to the full. There were opportunities there that were just not available in the home countries and the craze to get to America by all means possible became uppermost in the minds of many young Latinos from Central and South America as well as Africans and Asians.

A case in mind is the brazen attempt by Cuban youths to risk their lives by crowding themselves in boats and sailing out through shark-infested seas just to get away from the situation back home. More recently, there have been reports of hundreds of immigrants from Africa trying to go across the Mediterranean Sea to Europe but drowning in the process while in the South Pacific, we have read countless media reports of Asians similarly drowning in their efforts to get to Australia. Thousands of young people have lost their lives in the process. Many who have managed to get over have been arrested and either repatriated or locked up for months or years in detention centres. The majority of young people who have had this traumatic experience have completely lost their sense of direction in life and are never able to pick themselves up and start all over again, on getting back to their countries of origin. Many of them who manage to get to their cherished destinations discover soon after that the utopia of their dreams is a mirage – without contacts or friends, they are entirely on their own and before they know it, are on the streets, scavenging for food.

Only a small proportion of the young people who have tried have been successful because of the stringent immigration laws and procedures that they have to comply with. Recently, truck loads of Asian nationals smuggled in to the UK have been found on motorways and as one would expect, most have ended up being detained or sent back to their home countries. Very many have attempted avoiding being sent back by claiming to be political refugees – most European points of entry now have centres for pro-cessing such cases; these are virtual prisons or in a more acceptable term, detention centres, from which movement outside is restricted. Many somehow manage to get out and literally disappear into the system while others opt to be deported after months in these centres.

There are probably no statistics available in any developing country to establish how many young people apply to leave their countries of birth or those who actually leave and settle abroad or those who leave and get sent back. However taken as a whole the number of youngsters from developping countries that are repatriated annually while trying to gain access to Europe and the US/Canada must be staggering; it is hardly ever reported that the countries to which young people are repatriated lodge any form of complaint or take up the matter with the European or American government concerned. The feeling apparently that it is the fault of the travellers themselves and so is no problem of the government. However, governments in these countries need to be made aware that the problems of these youths arise from the lack of opportunities for them due to bad governance. The question thus arises therefore whether it is wrong or criminal for a young person in the developing world, who sees no opportunity for self-improvement at home, to attempt to emigrate to greener pastures abroad, often without genuine documents? If one may ask, what constitutes a genuine document for travel? It would obviously be right to assume that a travel document is not genuine if in the process of obtainnnning it, a false declaration is made, or a non-genuine document is used or a wrong age, address, marital status or name is declared, etc.

Everyone who has travelled abroad knows only too well that it is possible or unwise to answer very truthfully or correctly all questions that appear on a travel document. By this is meant that truthfully declaring what is asked may result in the applicant being denied a travel document or in delays in processing their papers. To avoid this, a traveller suffering from a serious bout of malaria puts the answer 'no' in columns where he/she is asked if he/ she suffers from the disease. He/she gets her travel document and later goes over the episode with glee when discussing with their friends, how they 'beat the system'. The friends get the idea and go on to enter fictitious answers in their travel forms. The point is that the person who makes a false declaration [by concealing material facts] and the one who tries to sneak over the border into another country by avoiding immigration, both commit the same offence. Based on this, it is reasonable to state that most of those who have migrated in the last 50 years to Europe or North America or New Zealand/Australia have, in all probabilities, had to lie about one material fact or another, to gain entry, though today, no one would admit it. The bottom line is that in many of the countries of the developped world, many of those who enforce immigration, have, in all probabilities, been themselves involved in breaking one immigration law or the other, themselves. If this is true, then one needs to ask whether it is fair and logical for such people to now be sitting in judgement over new immigrants wanting to do exactly what these people did to improve their lot in life.

It is not being suggested here that the boundaries or points of entry into the developed countries be thrown open to everyone from anywhere in the world – this would lead to immigration on a scale that cannot be controlled or managed. Rather, the argument is that far too many and unnecessary obstacles are today being placed in the way of young people from developing countries travelling to Europe or North America. And then, there is the matter of separate queues for immigration control when the aircraft gets to their destination. It is high time that leaders of developing countries begin to demand fair treatment for all their people at all entry points in Europe and North America. On a daily basis there are incidents of travellers seeking entry to these countries being maltreated, strip-searched, detained or deported immediately. A case in point is the Indian diplomat strip-searched at a US entry airport, which has generated ugly incidents and a backlash against US interests in India.

The world is now a global village and the United Nations needs to work towards achieving equal treatment for all and make it a goal to be achieved in the next ten years. Immigration counters need not be segregated because it sends a very depressing message to first-time visitors; it may have been necessary in pre-electronic age but not anymore. With biometric passports being the norm in most countries, all passengers on any one flight should be able to go through immigration in one single file, without the need to segregate. The present method should be phased out as it is old-fashioned and archaic. However, this may never happen if leaders of developing countries do not demand it, so the responsibility lies on their shoulders.

One other issue that strikes a wrong chord is the matter of visas for travel. It is rather interesting to note that, citizens of Europe, North America, Australia and New Zealand have exemptions from the requirement to obtain travel visas when travelling wi- thin their group of countries. Perhaps this is down to mutual agreement between the countries but the question arises as to why no Asian,

African or South American countries are ever granted the same exemptions and included on the lists. Or is it the case that none of these countries have ever applied to placed on the lists? Or have they applied and been rejected? On what criteria are the lists drawn up? Race, skin pigmentation, income-per-capita or GDP of the countries? Or has it got to do with considerations of health and control of infectious diseases from these less-advantaged countries? Or perhaps it is down to fears that travellers from the countries in question will overstay their visa times. It is always quite annoying to find cases where any one particular group of people is given blanket cover to do something which is denied another group. Or do third world leaders not see the point here in making an argument for their people?

Consider this quotation;

The earth is the Lord's and everything in it
The world and all who dwell in it

Many in the secular world do not believe that the earth is the Lord's but for those who believe, which are a majority, it is generally believed that when God created the world, there were no boundaries created. Nations and boundaries are the results of in- ability of people to live with one another and share. It is worth noting that Caucasian people did not begin, from day one, to in- habit the portion of the earth now referred to as Europe. It was only after centuries of migration that they found themselves settling down and over long periods of time, establishing their own states and nations, out of which grew the modern-day countries of Germany, France, Italy, etc, with lines demarcating the boundaries between them. In the same way, there were mass movements to Africa and Asia with the people creating nation states which, with European interventions, also took on statehood. So, today, we have in Africa and Asia, a duplication of the practice of modern nation states, all separated by boundaries.

There is no doubt that the first batch of European immigrants to America worked very hard to build the modern nations known as the United States and Canada. However it must not be forgotten these people were not the original inhabitants; they migrated, to escape forms of hardships in their original home- lands. It is a well-known fact that due to the poor potato harvests, hunger, large family sizes and unemployment that pervaded in Ireland several hundred years, many were driven to migrate to North America and settle down. It can rightly be stated that almost 90% of modern-day citizens of the US and Canada are immigrants or children of immigrants, who were escaping hunger, war, persecution, civil strife and the like. This is exactly what third world people are doing today.

The United States and Canada have very vast expanses of land that can still accommodate millions of immigrants. It is a good thing that both countries are actively encouraging emigration from Latin America, Africa and Asia. It is the view of this writer that they can do a lot more – 50,000 green cards the US is offering annually to would-be immigrants can conveniently be increased to 500,000. Leaders of developing countries should, as part of their international diplomatic functions, ask for the recommended increase and get the United Nations to back up the demand. A quota of say, 25,000 citizens from each developing country, should under UN guidelines, be allowed to emigrate yearly to either the United States, Canada, Australia or New Zealand, to escape hunger, malnutrition, disease, inter-tribal wars, etc. The UN should actually encourage and assist with such movements. In the same vein, Europeans, North Americans and Australians/New Zealanders who wish to emigrate to Asia or Africa or Central/South America should equally be encouraged and assisted to do so. It is the writer's belief that the world will benefit more from such free movements of people than the current practice of strictly restricting entry to developed countries for people from third world countries. The idea does need to be put across at the UN by third world leaders.

CHAPTER FIVE

TIME TO GIVE BACK STOLEN BOOTY

The first part of this chapter has been reproduced by kind per mission of the Voice, [Sept 17, 1996] a London weekly newspaper. The article featured Jewish goods and gold bullion confiscated by the Nazis and also a Bini [Nigerian] mask taken by the British expeditionary force in 1897 from the ancient Benin City. It followed demands at the time for the return to the Jews from Swiss banks of the gold looted by the Nazis, from them.

When does the Statute of Limitation run out on the crimes of the past? After ten years or 20 within the lifetime of those that the crimes were perpetrated against?

The issue is in the news again as the Foreign Office and Jewish groups attack the Swiss banking system following the publication of an official government report which accuses the Swiss of hoarding stolen Nazi gold worth a staggering £366 million in 1945 [£4 billion in late 90's].

This week [british] Foreign Secretary, the Swiss' behaviour. Labour MP Grenville Janner, whose original request led to the compilation of the document, was more vocal in his denunciations of the Swiss behaviour. He is quoted as saying, "The Swiss, from the report, clearly behaved in a thoroughly unworthy way during the war."

He went on to say that whether the gold came from individuals or was plundered from the national banks of the countries that the Nazis overran, the gold was stolen property and a respectable liberal democratic country like Switzerland ought not to be in the business of handling stolen goods.

Janner is not the only one who feels this way. Most of the commentators on radio and television have said more or less the same thing. Most have been outraged and have urged that something be done. Even the American government expects the Swiss to toe the line – and though no threat of sanctions has yet been made [or, perish the thought, military action such as the launching of cruise missiles] it is expected that all sorts of pressure will be brought to bear on the Swiss.

The problem is the same one that confronts all large claims of this sort, namely, who does the money go to? Assuming that the Jewish survivors who had the gold extracted from their mouths or stolen from their houses can be traced, then presumably the money can go straight to them. And likewise, if their descendants or the descendants of those who perished in the concentration camps can be identified, then again they should presumably be given back the money.

But how can they prove their claim? If the Nazis were butchering people in the barbarous manner that they were, is it fair to assume that the last thing they would have been handing out would have been receipts for the stolen gold?

However, to do nothing is to collude and endorse the barbarism and to ignore the gaping need for justice to right the wrongs of the past and to settle the rightful demands of the present.

So how do you move forward? Perhaps the Swiss could make a contribution to the compensation settlement of £4 billion, not to individual Jews but to charities and groups that work on behalf of Jewish interests. Or they could dedicate it to a particular programme, such as an educational programme that might benefit Jewish students. Maybe the state of Israel could have her Swiss debts to these banks written off and, if there aren't any debts, be given soft loans with no interests.

Either one of these options could right the wrongs of the past and settle the lingering hurt and offence of the present. They would acknowledge that the Swiss, through greed and a lack of human empathy, behaved in a way they ought not to have done. It would show the Swiss redeeming themselves for the wrongs of their past.

Whatever is done, we have to await it with baited anticipation since we know that when the British and Americans start huffing and getting on their moral high horse the way they are now, then something will be done.

Whichever action is chosen will be an interesting precedent – to be studied and used at a later date as part of the campaign to reclaim the numerous artefacts [works of art] stolen from the African [and other] continents du- ring the period of colonialism and slavery which are currently residing in various British museums and private collections, including the Queen's.

Of course we all know that when the campaign for repatriation makes its case the very same people denouncing the Swiss will probably turn round and say that there is no comparison – that the British case is more complex, that the artefacts were not stolen, that in any case they are being looked after properly in British museums since most of these African countries are not in a position to look after their own art treasures. We will hear all of this, as we have heard it in the past. However, the demands will not go away, since they are based on an injustice that will not be stilled until it is righted.

This stuff was stolen. The people who owned it did not give them away. They were taken away from them against their wishes — the definition of stealing. The British Museum and other collectors which have artefacts are in receipt of and are handling stolen goods. They can dress it up in whatever language they like but it doesn't change the facts. As the saying goes, the higher the monkey climbs, the more of its tail you see…

In the bottom right hand column of the article was a piece titled 'Crack-down long overdue', which went on as follows;

Why there should have been any surprise that the Swiss banking system is handling stolen goods beggars belief. Since the 60's it has been the biggest recipient of stolen money from various African and southern [third world] world dictators.

They have cloaked their involvement in laundering much of this money through their so-called secrecy laws, which is nothing more than a thieves' charter. Perhaps while they are at it the Americans and British will insist that the Swiss reform their banking system and in cases where dictators have dipped into their national treasuries and illegally siphoned off money to Swiss banks the Swiss [banks] be made to repay [refund] the money.

In this country [Britain] the receiver of stolen goods is treated more harshly than the thief – on the basis that if the demand didn't exist, then the thief would not be so active. Swiss banking 'fences' should be cracked down on equally hard.

COMMENTS

Two issues of relative importance to all third world countries have been touched upon by Onyekachi Wambu in the above article – the treasures and works of art stolen from them during colonial times and the very serious matter of Switzerland [and, to a lesser extent, some other European countries] providing a safe haven for greedy third world leaders and their loot. There has been a lot said about the billions of dollars stolen from their nations' treasuries by the late Ferdinard Marcos of the Philippines and the self-styled Mobutu Sese-Seko of Zaire [Congo] as well as the army general Abacha of Nigeria which are deposited in the vaults of Swiss banks. Unfortunately for the people of these three countries, the people concerned, who alone know the total amount of their nations' wealth that they have managed to 'salt away' in their names, are dead. Alas! But the wealth remains, sadly in the Swiss banking and financial system, oiling it and keeping it going, with much of it going out again as loans to the very countries from which the money came in the first place; paradoxically interests on the loans are going to the banks, to further swell then system. So, in a nutshell, until the end of time, the Swiss economy will continue to thrive on their gains from these deposits of ill-gotten wealth.

The above raises an issue. Are there not people in Switzerland, with some conscience, who can stand up and say, 'Enough of stolen money in our system!'? Well if the Swiss will not do it because they are benefitting from it, why have third world leaders all kept mute about this crime to their people? Is there not enough poverty and suffering in the third world caused in part by these heinous practices and bad governance for the crop of current leaders of third world countries to begin to pressurize Switzerland to stop accepting their stolen wealth? It is widely believed that because of corruption at high levels in governance in third world countries, no serious demands may ever be made to either the Swiss government or the World Bank or the United nations for a halt to be put to the Swiss banking system which is encouraging third world leaders to steal and convert to their use, half their nations' wealth. If this is the case, then perhaps only a pressure group of people such as lawyers, university lecturers, accountants and philanthropists from these countries getting together and setting up a forum to effect as change will do. Switzer land, and for that matter, other countries providing safe havens for the stolen treasuries of the third world should be stopped in their tracks because they are committing serious crimes against humanity. They can be held partly accountable for the hundreds of thousands of cases of third world people suffering from malnutrition, poverty, disease and homelessness in these countries today, never mind what they are trying to do, with the Red Cross. It is a case of taking with both hands from a people and giving back with two fingers.

The Swiss are keeping in their systems money that is meant to provide housing, food, good roads, health-care, electricity and employment for these people; there are no two ways of looking at it! It is a crime against humanity and the Swiss need to be told, bluntly. How, indeed, do the Swiss feel, knowing that they are keeping and utilizing such money, when they hear of hunger and starvation and abject poverty in these countries? Or worse still, do not have any qualms about extracting interests on loans from these countries, on money that is rightfully theirs? Or do the Swiss have no morals whatsoever? If not, then it is about time that all third world countries begin to boycott Swiss products [consider Rolex watches and chocolate, for a start], until they put an end to the crime they are perpetrating against their people.

Next on the issue are artefacts. Perhaps the problem for third world leaders today in trying to recover these objects is that if they press too hard for their return, they would perhaps lose out on aid packages promised them by the countries holding on to the artefacts. It has been said earlier that if only third world countries would put their houses and finances in order, they would not be needing the aid packages, because they do not amount to much, really. It would appear that not enough pressure have been put on the countries holding on to the artefacts to release them; perhaps, if the leaders themselves will not do it, then the pressure group earlier mentioned, should begin to put the case across, say at the UN.

In the final analysis, if the countries holding on to the objects are determined to hold on to them, then maybe they can be made to 'buy' them at a price to be set by the original countries from which they came, taking into consideration the market value of the individual items. Though this would sound like a sacrilege [selling off the items] it would appear the only option if they would not be handed back mutually. It does not appear that either now, or in the foreseeable future is any third world country going to have the stomach or the means to go to war to settle the dispute. So they might as well negotiate for them to be sold and, from the proceeds, replicas of the items can be reproduced and displayed in their national museums. This may well be the honourable way out. Alternatively, replicas can be made for the museums in the countries where they are held and the originals returned to their home countries, as a gesture of goodwill.

Perhaps a recent article in Yahoo.com news [03/01/2014] titled 'Slavery links to UK stately Homes Revealed' takes the case for remuneration for resources [in this case, human] forcibly taken and sold, one level higher. In the said article by Samantha Payne[Dec 28 2013] it is claimed that the link between Britain's stately homes and African slavery has been repressed, according to a new book which explores how the slave trade helped wealthy [slave] owners built their country estates. It goes on to say that over 100 country houses and estates across the UK benefitted from the millions of pounds given in compensation to slave owners in the 19th century – when slave ownership was abolished in Britain in 1833, the government paid out a total of £20million – the equivalent of £16.5billion today – to compensate thousands of wealthy families for the loss of their 'property'!! The database from which the above is compiled shows who had slave-related property at the time of emancipation, but some landowners had moved out of slavery by the time it was abolished.

The issues raised by the above are many. Firstly, how right was it that it was to the slave trading families, rather than the nation states from which the slaves were taken, that compensation was paid? Who were the families that benefitted? Knowing how well records are kept in Britain, it should be very possible to establish which families gained. Is there not a good case for these families to be made to refund the present equivalent of their total profits from slave trading, for onward forwarding to the countries from which the bulk of the slaves in the Atlantic trade were taken? A further question that can be asked is, how fair is it for these families to continue to keep the proceeds of such heinous trade, in this day and age? Call it reparation or compensation, the countries from which they were taken deserve to be given back some remuneration for the ignoble trade in humans. Again as with other matters, it remains for the leaders from the countries concerned to raise the matter at the appropriate place and time, for it to be considered.

CHAPTER SIX

THE PROBLEM OF LEADERSHIP

Undoubtedly, the greatest problem for many third world countries is bad leadership. In order for us to know what this is, let us look at good leadership, which is its flip side (assuming it is a record). Good leadership or governance for any nation is the ability, willingness and dedication to deliver to the people what is promised them when assuming power. Essentially this means a good administration, transparent honesty, proper use of the country's financial, economic and human resources, resulting in adequate or near-adequate provision for the people of good housing, roads, potable water, electricity, employment, law and order, security, quality education, etc, while at the same time creating an enabling environment for individuals to set up and run enterprises that will help boost the economy. That is about all that is required of governments. If this is the case, then why is it that the majority of third world governments are unable to deliver these essentials, with all the resources at their disposal? More-so in those ones that have been blessed with limitless re- sources.

The questions raised by the above are many. If it can be done reasonably well in the developed countries what stops third world countries from being able to? Is the problem with the type of governments practised or with the people who are leading? Or is it that the people are inherently incapable of leader- ship? What actually drives and motivates people to want to lead in these countries? Is it something to boost their ego or to gain self-aggrandisement? Is it greed or love of power or just seeking an opportunity to enrich themselves? Could it be that there is a real desire to improve the lot of their countrymen and women, thereby ensuring progress?

Why is it that, whether it be civilian or military, many third world governments are just not delivering. The irony of it all is that, every so often, there is an election or military intervention and the people all hail a new government but at the end of the day, fails to deliver. This cycle of affairs has gone on for so ma- ny decades in many third world countries and nothing seems to be able to break it. Governments come and governments go and those who run them benefit immensely but deliver very little. Must this go on for ever? Must the change of baton continue from one poor performer to another or is it time to stop and ponder what has gone wrong for decades and try and map out a new course?

This writer has lived in the United Kingdom for nearly 30 years and in all that time, he has never gone into the bathroom to find that there was no water; the WC has flushed every time he has pulled the lever. The light has gone off just twice – once in 1987 when the great hurricane swept away many trees across motor roads and over electricity cables and in 2011 when an electricity supply depot was broken into by copper-wire thieves! No matter how far a house is from a town, it had electric and water supply. Dysentery is unheard of. Occasionally he has seen potholes on a few roads; most roads in towns and cities are swept and the rubbish bins are emptied. Lifts in buildings work and no matter how high on a high-rise building one goes, there is always running water. One never goes into a supermarket to find that there is no bread or milk or rice (rice is not grown in the UK!). There is never petrol rationing or food rationing (not since the end of the war). Gas, which is piped to most homes, is never in short supply, considering that the majority of UK homes today use gas for cooking and heating their homes. Food is relatively affordable for most people. And of course, people pay their taxes (PAYE and Council) and these are put to good use, this being the main source of revenue for the government. In short, the system here works. It would be right to conclude that, specifically for this reason, many people have migrated from the third world countries to the UK, Europe, North America and other places where facilities are functional.

A survey would show every time that many third world people living in developed countries would rather be in their native countries if the system worked in them. Many of them may live abroad for decades but they never really settle in and always yearn for that time when they can return, that is, when things back home, would improve. However, with the way things are going in their home countries and many hundreds of thousands more planning to move abroad, one question that readily shoots up is how long third world people must wait for their leaders to sort out the mess in their countries.

Let us look at water supply. Is it not such a shame that after 50 years of self-rule, a government minister in charge of water resources in Nigeria has been quoted as saying that the government cannot provide the people potable water! If one considers that if only 10% of all the revenue that Nigeria has earned from oil in the last 20 years were invested in water supply, there is absolutely no reason why there would not be adequate water and certainly, water would be available in all floors of buildings. This would ensure better sanitation and health. However the government seems to have given up on the problem of water supply and electricity because the problems seem to have grown out of proportion, as a result of population explosion. Whatever is being budgeted for these utilities seem to be going down the drain or personal bank accounts. The issue is, what happens to the people who misuse or embezzle such funds? They go away with their ill-gotten money and buy themselves expensive cars and acquire more wives and concubines and then 'spray' [throw money at] performers and dancers at lavish parties, and surprise, surprise, get awarded chieftaincy titles by their local chiefs. On top of this, three things happen – the intended project is not executed, the 'contractor' gets off with his/her 'loot' and the people for whom it is intended suffer.

The above is not to say that there are no third world countries where people are genuinely making some effort to improve the lot of their people. The fact is that if the problem is not mal-administration, it is corruption or greed or inefficiency or a combination of one or all. Whatever it is, it appears that development is taking far too long to get to the great majority of third world people and for no fault of theirs. The cycle could go on for another 50 or 100 years and there is not going to be much difference from the way things presently are. There will still be abject poverty and under-development in many of these countries whether they are blessed with resources or not. Governments here have failed woefully to bring development to the people and so a new way out needs to be found if so-called leaders are not going to continue to take them on a ride.

What is being proposed here is a fresh approach to the issue of development in third world and developing countries. As it appears that 'local contractors' have been unsuccessful for many decades now to provide water, electricity, roads , hospitals and infrastructure in these countries, perhaps it is high time the services are contracted out to foreign companies. It is quite certain that if Thames Water for example, were asked to sort out the water problem in Nigeria and are given just about the same amount of money as these 'contractors' are getting and squandering, it would not take them five years before they put things in order. The same can be said of NPower looking into the perennial electricity problem of Nigeria. In the same vein, some German or French company can look into the problem of roads and Italians, telephone. Let the governments pay them on contract basis and over a 5-year period, we shall begin to see a big change in the direction in which progress and development will come to these beleaguered countries.

The above proposals may appear far-fetched or smack of neo- colonialism but the time has come for the kind of option to be considered. Let it be done on contract basis – pay the foreign companies a fee but set some parameters and controls, like ensuring that local labour is utilised. Two things are certain. They will do a good job and they will not disappear with the money. That is in sharp contrast with what currently happens, with the job not being done and the money disappearing, with nothing being done about it. It appears to be time the business of governance is taken more seriously.

It is pertinent to observe at this point that while Nigeria has been identified as a case in point, much of what has been stated as happening in Nigeria is equally the case in many of the third world or developing countries. One is left no option but to ask if the problem is with the leaders chosen or the method of choosing them or the people they have to work with. This may well not be the case. The main problem appears to be that the leaders have never had any parameters within which to operate, other than the 'oath' they swear – they have never truly been answerable to their people. In every sense therefore, they have come unto the arena, played the game any way they wished, and gone off with whatever result they got, no questions asked. In most cases they have left the scene in a more pitiable state than they met it, but never empty-handed themselves. They and their cohorts have always ensured that adequate provision has been made for their future and those of their children. And, they have always gotten away with their 'booties'. The time for an end to be put to this has come.

As a lesson in how to provide good governance free of corruption and embezzlement of state funds, it is difficult, if we look at developed economies, to find cases of former leaders who turn billionaires while in office, or even after leaving. Because they are fully aware of the need for probity and accountability, they operate within the parameters set and remain accountable at all times while in office. In the same manner when they award con- tracts, whoever wins such contracts knowing that they are under scrutiny, ensures that they are performed, satisfactorily. Most contracts have very generous margins for profit but when every contractor eyes not just the profit but 75% or more of the total sum, then something is seriously wrong.

In a previous chapter, mention has been made of the very vast amounts of money deposited in accounts in developed countries by third world leaders who have 'fleeced' their systems; many have invested their loot in expensive mansions abroad [that they rarely live in] and sent their children to educational establish-ments in these countries. One thing they fail to remember how-ever is that the children will always be misfits either in the fo-reign countries where they are educated or in their home coun-tries. So at the end of the day, it is well worth asking by these 'leaders' if it is in their children's interest to 'ship' them abroad while running their home country aground.

Building Anti-Corruption Agencies in the African Commonwealth

Blog

By Guest on 5 June 2014 in Aid and Development

George Appiah

Frank Vogl is a founding member of Transparency International and the author of *Waging War on Corruption – Inside the Movement Fighting the Abuse of Power*. He blogs at: http://frankvogl.com/ethics-world/

Anti-Corruption Agencies (ACAs) have been established in increasing numbers of countries in recent years and have complemented the efforts by public prosecutors and the judiciary to curb corruption in their countries. Are they making a difference?

The unanimous view of the heads of 17 ACAs from African countries that are members of the Commonwealth is a resounding yes. Meeting in Accra, Ghana, last week at the invitation of the Commonwealth Secretariat, these leaders argued that they are making significant progress. At the same time, they voiced concern that they are not being given enough credit for their achievements.

In the course of a four-day closed-door conference the leaders of the ACAs spoke candidly about their achievements and their shortcomings. There was no evidence of complacency. Many of the ACAs are acutely aware that they are walking a very fine political line. If they are too bold and go after what were continually referred to as "the big fish" they knew that they risked having their agencies closed down. If the ACAs, on the other hand, only concentrated on rather low-level matters of corruption, then they would be widely viewed as lacking in political independence and they would fail to garner essential public support.

Drilling deeply into the work of individual ACAs it becomes apparent that many of them have been building effective alliances with other law enforcement agencies in their countries and increasingly concentrating their efforts on areas where they believe they can have an impact. Some ACAs are building records of significant asset recovery. Others are engaging in high profile cases, such as corruption in land management that can involve ordinary citizens, major business enterprises and national and municipal authorities. Others are striving to work with judges to ensure that significant anti-corruption cases are fast-tracked to the courts and not left for years to languish.

At the same time, many of the officials attending the conference were concerned about international indexes that portrayed their countries as highly corrupt. Transparency International's Corruption Perceptions Index was a particular target. In sum, some of the officials suggested that they work hard all year to strengthen anti-corruption initiatives in their countries, then along comes the CPI with a score that suggests things may actually be getting worse in their countries. The ACAs want more credit and recognition for their work.

To achieve this, however, will demand an array of actions. The ACAs need to build highly skilled teams of investigators and anti-corruption experts and here the Commonwealth Secretariat has taken an important initiative in establishing a training centre in Botswana. Moreover, conferences like the one in Accra last week help the leaders of ACAs to build informal networks where they can exchange information and ideas throughout the year with colleague in other countries facing similar practical problems.

The ACAs need to work hard to build their public credibility and be seen as politically independent. Ultimately their authority over time will depend on public trust and public support. Some of the officials at the meeting asserted that this is difficult when the media itself is corrupt, or the tool of corrupt business people and politicians. The argument is for the ACAs in part to strengthen their communications skills, being more pro-active, reaching out more to work with civil society inn their countries and to be seen as more transparent and accountable.

The work of the ACAs would be greatly strengthened in many countries if the governments of those countries passed effective freedom of information laws, laws that gave meaningful protection to whistleblowers, and laws that demanded comprehensive asset declarations by individuals seeking electoral office.

In informal discussions on the side of the conference I found a number of officials willing to admit that they were deeply concerned about corruption in the military and in the security forces in their countries. They acknowledged that while corruption in this sector is almost certainly significant, the remit of ACAs does not reach as far as areas that are considered "national security."

Governments of all countries need to confront the reality that no public sector area should enjoy impunity: all need to be subject to effective public oversight. Barring anti-corruption agencies from investigating defence sector contracting and the uses of public funds for security purposes undermines the credibility of governments that claim that they are fighting corruption.

This is an issue likely to come more into the foreground in coming months and years as it becomes more widely recognized that there are close corruption linkages between human insecurity, national security and international security. As we have seen with the Taliban in Afghanistan and Pakistan, and with Boko Haram in Nigeria, insurgent groups win support from the poor whose lives are miserable thanks in part to corruption, whose anger with officials who routinely extort bribes is palpable and who feel powerless to defend themselves against abuse. The poor see their government as their enemy, not as their protector. Radical terrorist groups take advantage of this discontent to win supporters.

In many countries in sub-Saharan Africa the ACAs are striving to counter the widespread corruption in their countries. The Commonwealth deserves credit for working with the ACAs to encourage their efforts, to assist them to learn from diverse country experiences and share knowledge, and to improve staff training.

About Guest

The TI-UK blog features thought and opinion from guest writers as well as TI staff. Any opinions expressed by external contributors do not necessarily reflect the views of Transparency International UK.

Share on emailShare on printMore Sharing ServicesShare

Transparency International UK is a chapter of

Having come this far, it is pertinent to ask at this point what parameters need to be set. It is apparent that the time has come for people in third world and developing countries to be setting stringent rules for all citizens who aspire to leadership as president, prime minister, governor, minister, senator, local government chairman, etc. These should include;

a] declarations of all material wealth owned, before swearing in.

b] declarations, sworn to, that while in office, they will not indulge in promoting their personal wealth c] declarations that they will devote all their working time to fin- ding solutions to the problems in areas they are overseeing.

d] declarations that at all times, their private financial dealings are open to scrutiny by relevant government bodies.

e] declarations that they will not operate or participate in, or have any interest in any business or utilize others for same.

f] signed agreements to deposit with a relevant government body, monthly statement of their accounts - [none abroad].

g] declarations that they will not receive financial or material rewards from any beneficiary of government contracts with whom they have dealt.

h] declarations that they will accept no gifts in the form of money or property or land, while in office.

i] sign an undertaking that if found to have contravened any of the above to resign their appointments forthwith or be removed.

To enable them cope with the above constraints, the families of presidents, prime ministers and governors should be catered for by the government while such people are in office. That means that their children would be educated at state expense, to remove the burden from the office holders; the number of children can be pegged. Everything for ensuring that the office holder is able to perform his/her tasks should be provided them though opulence in any form should be avoided. Foreign trips and social functions must be reduced to an absolute minimum – prudence in the use of resources must be the watchword. Once this cycle is set and begins, as it were [like a machine] to function or rotate, it should keep going. The essence would be lead - by example. Let every third world and developing country leadership aspirant agree to subject him/herself to the above constraints if they truly want to serve their people. There is absolutely no doubt that the above will ensure the elimination of all forms of mal-practices in the higher echelons of governance and the delivery of the good proceeds of democracy to the people.

At the end of the president/minister/governor's term in office, it should be quite an easy task for the people to tell if he/she did well. The evidence will be there for everyone to see. For those groups of leaders who perform well and raise standards, a lump sum [say, about $100,000 – 250, 000, depending on how rich the country is] should be paid out to them at the end of their term of office, where it can be shown that they have delivered and quality of life has improved. Before this is done a final statement and declaration must be made, detailing their wealth, when leaving office; perhaps for presidents, prime ministers and governors, this should be published, for all to see and should become standard practice. No doubt, this will discourage many specula- tors aspiring to lead but with the ulterior motive of enriching themselves while in office. The lesson in all this, for third world and developing countries leaders and people is that reward is not to be taken [or given] upfront; it is only due after the work is done. It is hoped the point is understood.

Though it may be argued that the above proposal is a trespass on human rights, it need be stated that the situation in many third world and developing countries today is drastic, with many people migrating and suffering from malnutrition, poverty and disease that over 50 years of misrule have heaped on hapless citizens of these countries. Drastic situations call for drastic solutions. It is disheartening for people from these countries in the developed economies watching newsreels and videos of their people going through the degrading and inhuman experiences of boat mishaps trying to cross to greener pastures. The trend needs to be stopped and there is no better way.

In any case no one who aspires to lead is compelled to accept the above conditions or suggestions. However, anyone who genuinely wants to lead should have no qualms with doing them. Over a period of time, once the idea of accountability has become 'in-grafted' as it were in the system, then the constraints may be removed, piecemeal.

Let every third world and developing country leadership aspirant rise up to and accept the above challenge, before being consider-ed for leadership and we shall find the unusually long list of aspirants in every country drastically reduced. Among those who are left, the task of choosing worthy leaders and policing their activities once they are elected becomes a lot easier. Only very minimal checks and balances will be necessary. Not only will it become easier to keep national resources in government coffers and use them prudently, it will also begin to build in the people in general and future aspirants in particular, the right attitude to leadership.

It is a well-known fact that any leader who performs well does not need to embezzle money while in office – after he/she has left office, the good work they have done will do the talking for them and ensure that, for the rest of their lives and for their families and off-springs, they will not only have enough to live on, but will leave untarnished names for posterity. The third world and developing countries are today full of ex-leaders who cannot hold their heads high and without shame and declare that the wealth they own is not ill-gotten.

Once the right calibre of people can be brought together in any setting in these countries, based on the parameters set above, then the problem of leadership will be half-solved. Where will the other half of the solution come from? This will be in the area of delivery. There is no gainsaying the fact that corrupt as governments might appear to be in third world and developing countries, they still go ahead and award contracts for one project or the other, pay out contract money only to find that the projects are poorly executed or not at all. Sadly, they have been powerless in chasing after the culprits, who would have put the money to their own use or in the pursuit of pleasure. Many government contracts have always been awarded to cohorts of corrupt leaders but with the above recommendations, these type of people will disappear because leaders will have no need of them. Only people who are qualified professionally and who pass rigorous selection criteria will sail through the process of contract awards; they must also not only deliver but meet dead-lines. Contract amounts should be paid out in stages based on progress made by those executing projects. The era of friends, in-laws, college-mates or pretty women who know nothing about drainage being awarded ten-figure sum contracts for drainage in town and city centres will become a thing of the past.

Being above board therefore, is the first and most important requisite for any aspiring leader in the third world and developing countries, if the problems of the region are ever to be resolved.

CHAPTER SEVEN

GATHERING STUBBLE

So the people scattered all over Egypt to gather stubble to use for straw...
Exodus 5, 12.

In biblical times, it is recorded that thousands of Israelites, as a result of hunger and famine in Israel, migrated to Egypt and became virtual slaves. It became their lot to gather stubble which was used for straw which at the time was used for making bricks that were used in the construction of palaces, cities and perhaps the pyramids. It was obviously hard and tedious work, considered too menial for the Egyptians [who were lording it over them] but fitting for the Israelites.

It is a well-known fact that after the world wars, many people from the under-developed world were encouraged to migrate to Europe to provide cheap labour for the vast reconstruction and rehabilitation work necessary to rebuild the cities and railways, destroyed by Hitler's Luftwaffe. Their lot was to dig, lift, transport, and clear in the rebuilding process. In effect, they did work similar to what the Israelites were compelled to do in Egypt during their stay there. Through their sweat and labour, the great rail tracks, industrial complexes, roads, bridges and housing projects were constructed.

Many Semites, according to Simon Sebag Montefiore, in his book, Jerusalem, the Biography, settled in Egypt and Ramses the
Great was probably the pharaoh that compelled the Jews to work on his store-cities. This is where Moses received the revelation to lead the people from Egypt, to the promised land. He was a charismatic leader of the Jews.

Yemen migrant boat sinking is 'worst this year' - UN

Thousands make the dangerous journey every year
Continue reading the main story

Migrant tragedy

- [**Mapping the routes**](#)
- [**Q&A: Migrants and asylum**](#)
- [**'Easier from Libya'**](#)
- [**Survivor's ordeal**](#)

The UN's refugee agency reports that 62 people have died off Yemen's coast, in what it describes as the worst sinking incident in the region this year.

Sixty migrants from Somalia and Ethiopia and two Yemeni crew members drowned in the accident last weekend, the UNHCR said on Friday.

Every year thousands of Africans make the journey to Yemen in crowded boats.

Yemen is seen as a gateway to the Middle East or Europe but hundreds have died on the journey.

"The victims were reportedly buried by local residents after their bodies washed ashore near the Bab El Mandeb area off Yemen's coast," the UNHCR said in a statement.

The incident brings the number of people who have been killed trying to make this particular crossing this year to 121, the agency said.

Many thousands have fled the Horn of Africa in recent years to escape poverty and war.

The route to Europe via the Mediterranean Sea is also **heavily used**by migrants fleeing the Horn of Africa and, increasingly, refugees from the war in Syria.

From January to April, 42,000 migrants were detected on Mediterranean routes, with 25,650 of these crossing from Libya.

More on This Story
Migrant tragedy
Features and analysis

In moves similar to the above, many young and able-bodied people from the third world and developing countries, coming from an economically disadvantaged background, have, in the past several decades, been compelled to migrate to the developed countries of Europe and North America with the majority forced by circumstances to subject themselves to menial jobs such as

cleaning, bus and train driving, railway station maintenance, hospital porters, etc.

Up until relatively recently, the situation had not changed
much. In many developed countries, people from the less
developed countries who have migrated there find themselves operating at the lowest rungs of the ladder of employment; they clean the hospitals and streets, sell tickets at
train and bus stations, drive the buses and taxi-cabs, clean
the offices and toilets, attend to the sick in hospitals and
care-homes, sweat in the kitchens of hotels, take-aways and
restaurants [not making or serving the meals] but washing
the large cooking pots and utensils, dishes, cutleries and
floors, pick fruits on the farms and do all the menial jobs
available, just because such opportunities do not exist
where they come from, and usually for low wages. Because
of the very low wages, most have to work very long hours
to earn enough to live on.

For hundreds of thousands of these people, it is an uphill
struggle coping with these problems, in addition to having
to normalise they stay and bring up their families. Every
one of them is forever looking forward to the day when
they can get out of the vicious cycle, have adequate money
and return to their home countries. Many gamble on the
football pools and horse-racing and play the lottery and
some foolish ones take to drinking and drugs, to try and
bury their problems. For most of them, it is one tortuous
road to travel. While music and sports have provided a way
out for a number of them, the majority are still having a
very hard time and this is exacerbated by the racism which
they encounter, regularly.

There is basically nothing wrong with someone working hard to earn a living. Historically people from the developing countries have had to toil for everything they ever needed. For the majority, who are from a rural back ground, they have had to till the soil, often having to trek many kilometres from their dwellings and for most of the day labouring under the hot sun. For water, many have to resort to digging deep wells from which they draw up water or trek many kilometres to a stream or pool carrying the bowl of water on their heads or back. These are difficult tasks to perform and it becomes more difficult for many when they have to go up windy paths and hills to get home. The sad thing however is that most of the people from the developing countries who migrate to the developed nations do not come from this class, many having gone through the basic educational process of secondary and/or university courses. If all was right in their home countries, there would really not be any need for them to migrate in the first place.

It is rather pathetic to observe that among present-day migrants are engineers, doctors, accountants, lawyers, pharmacists and teachers educated in their home countries and who are forced to take up menial tasks in order to survive the first few years of their sojourn in developed countries. Many do not declare their full qualifications when applying for such jobs for fear they will be considered over-qualified and refused the jobs. The question that comes to mind is, do they have any better option or, for that matter, any option at all? The logical one is for them to leave all these behind and return to their home countries but herein lies the problem.

For many from the third world and developing countries, home is no place to go back to due to the total absence of facilities and infrastructure to make living worthwhile, a situation created in the main by those in power. Housing is non-existent; it is no secret that many of these people in the developed countries who enjoy the 'luxury' of 3-bed-room houses and flats left their home countries sharing single rooms with several cousins and other relatives. The transport infrastructure in most of the countries is poor and so are electricity, water supply, health-care and educa-tion. In nearly all the cases, it is all down to mal-admini-stration and corruption in high places and not because there is no money. It is so sad to see many third world leaders living in grand surroundings and opulence, when all around them is abject poverty and decay. How these 'leaders' can be so carefree is baffling. Many of them do not, in the least, deserve the lifestyle that they live, at the expense of their people. Why should they lead such comfortable lives when the people they lead do not? Far too much of the countries' revenue is being spent on making them comfortable. To buttress the point, which parent goes to a well-deserved rest on a cosy bed when their children have had no food or are sick? No responsible parent will.

The failure or unwillingness of many third world and develop- ing countries leaders to consider what their actions and inactions are causing for millions of the countrymen and women is a very heinous crime against humanity. Many of their people who leave home to seek greener pastures abroad are only compelled by circum-stances to do so. Little do they know what awaits them in the countries they travel to and in fact, many suffer the shock of what they encounter. If 85% of them were to be aware of what awaits them in the first 5 years of their sojourn in foreign lands, they will choose not to leave home. On arrival at the port of en- try, they are thoroughly screened and put through many embarrassing episodes of interrogation [with people on the queues be-hind them hearing every conversation with immigration officers, however personal]. If their motives for seeking entry are unclear, then heaven help them because they are often refused entry and put back on the next available plane to their home country. The ones among them who do sail through and are allowed access find out very soon that they have many obstacles to overcome – getting accom-modation, coping with the weather, coping with prejudice and racism, looking for work or starting a course, etc and dealing with the endless influx of bills that pour in through the letter box. There is no gainsaying the fact that these all lead, in no time, to social and psychological problems for migrants, from which many never recover. The blame for such problems can be safely put at the feet of their leaders who, in the first place, are creating the situations in their countries that compel people to emigrate.

The above is not to say that there are absolutely no migrants among these people who have benefited from migrating. Quite a percentage have gone on to acquire academic and professional qualifications while others have embarked on careers and businesses that have taken them in new directions and enabled them to make new and be-neficial contacts. However, taken as a whole the percen-tage of these people who fall into this category is perhaps in single figures, ie between 1 and 9 percent. Taken as part of the total number of migrants, one can safely say that migration generally has been more beneficial to the host nations than for the home countries, except one factors in the remittances sent home by the migrants. The point however needs to be made that if the right atmosphere and environment prevailed in the home countries, most of their citizens who migrate would achieve a great deal more in their home countries.

One sad aspect of the migration of third world and developing countries nationals is that these countries are lo-sing generations of potential leaders and workforce who would otherwise contribute to their growth, progress and development. This has been referred to as brain drain in which doctors, accountants, lawyers, nurses, etc who trained and qualified in their home countries are lured by the better pay and conditions abroad.

Responsible and committed leaders from these countries need to take this as a challenge, to see that corrupt leadership is phased out and replaced by good governance that brings with it transparency, accountability, true democracy, development and improvement in the lives of citizens. Only when this happens will people begin to take pride in being citizens of their countries and shun the desire to travel to other countries to improve their lot in life. Let the leaders put the people first and their own personal interests last and see how things will begin to take a turn for the better. If they look well after their countries first, then their countries will look after them; this should be the new deal and ideal, for the leaders.

CHAPTER EIGHT

WHAT ROLE EDUCATION?

Elliot and Atkinson [1998, pp 240-241] claim that what most people want from education may be described as 'security' – a reasonable pay in a good job, but this is a scenario that can no longer be guaranteed. The issue here is, is there a link between education and economic performance? Put another way, could heavy investments by developing countries in education have the effect that those educated will begin to impact the economy by dreaming and coming up with new products and ideas that can bring in economic gains to their countries?

Both people above argue further that it is not easy to see what the policy of education, education and education is actually go- ing to achieve and that on its own, raising educational standards will not be the magic ingredient that will ensure higher levels of growth. In their reasoning, the establishment of a training establishment for astronauts and rocket scientists would not necessarily ensure that Britain develops its own space programme. They go on to say that it is hard to find proof that links educational attainment with growth levels and buttress this by a study by Peter Robinson [LSE, 1997] which says that once the vast majority of the adult population is functionally literate, as in the developed countries, a link between the attainment of qualifications and economic performance is hard to demonstrate.

Could the above be said of developing countries? Can the attainment of qualifications be a spur for people here to aspire to the invention of new products and ideas that, with time, can be commercialized, to yield revenue for their countries? Or is it enough for them to just find themselves work, settle down and earn themselves a living, leaving all their knowledge to waste?

Let us look at the greatest inventors of the world and consider the role education played in their lives and inventions.

Top 10 Inventors of all Time

10 great inventors who helped change the world.

1. **Thomas Edison** (1847 – 1931)

Edison filed over 1,000 patents. He developed and innovated a wide range of products from the electric light bulb to the phonograph and motion picture camera.

2. **The Wright Brothers**

Successfully designed, built and flew the first powered aircraft, showing that man could fly. One of most important inventions of Twentieth Century.

3. **Benjamin Franklin** (1705 - 1790)

Polymath who discovered electricity and invented the Franklin stove

4. **Charles Babbage** (1791 – 1871)

- Created first mechanical computer, which proved to be the prototype for future computers. Considered to be the 'Father of Computers'

5. **James Watt** (1736 – 1819)

Inventor of the steam engine, which was critical in the industrial revolution. His invention of a separate condensing chamber, greatly improved the efficiency of steam.

6. **Alexander Bell** (1847 – 1922)

Credited with inventing the first practical telephone. Also worked on optical telecommunications, aeronautics and hydrofoils.

7.   **Leonardo Da Vinci** (1452 – 1519)

One of the greatest ever minds, invented models that proved workable 3-500 years later.

8.   **Galileo** (1564-1642)

Developed a powerful telescope and confirmed revolutionary theories about the nature of the world. Also developed an improved compass.

9.  **Tim Berners Lee**

Developed the http:// protocol for the internet. Making the world wide web freely available.

10.  **Archimedes** (287 BC – c. 212 BC)

Amongst other things worked out pi and developed the Archimedes screw for lifting up water from mines or wells.

View more: Famous inventors throughout history

Citation : Pettinger, Tejvan. "*Top 10 Inventors*", Oxford, www.biographyonline.net - 4th Sept. 2012.

Inventors and their Inventions

The question of whether formal education has any part to play in the making of inventors can be answered by looking at the background of some of those listed above.

Thomas Edison, a famous inventor in the area of electricity and light bulbs was mainly self-educated, having read Isaac Newton's 'Principa Mathematica' finding it too complicated and resolving to make science more understandable. He was, at 19, sponsored for training as a telegraph operator for Western Union in Louisville, Kentucky. He worked in experiments in chemistry and inventions, carried out over 3,000 theoretical studies about the electric light and started producing light bulbs with William Hammer, which became a great commercial success.

James Watt, famous for developing a separate condensing chamber for the steam engine that greatly improved its efficiency, was a Scottish inventor, mechanical engineer and chemist. His invention played a key role in the industrial revolution.

Charles Babage, born in 1791 in London, had many tutors and in 1810 was accepted at Trinity College, Cambridge to do ma- thematics and there came up with an idea to do calculations by machine, after he looked at some loga- rithms. In 1822, he began work on his 'difference engine' that sought to mechanically carry out calculations. In 1991, a new machine, using his design, was built and it became the precursor of modern computers.

Tim Berners-Lee, inventor of the world-wide web, went to Queens College, Oxford and studied physics. After gra- duating he worked for Plessey, a printing company in Poole and then became a contractor with CERN Switzer- land, where he began a project based on the use of 'hyper- text' language for sharing information with researchers in different locations. Hypertext put together all the techno- logy involved in the web. Working with Robert Caillian, in 1990 he produced the first version of the world –wide- web, the first web browser and the first web server.

John Atanason, who invented the first electronic digital computer, studied electrical engineering at University of Florida and then mathematics at Iowa State College for his masters and then PhD in theoretical physics at University of Wisconsin.

From the above, it is evident that education has greatly influenced progress in the area of inventions; apparently without it, there is no way the inventors listed above would have been able to achieve all they did.

It is a well-known fact that many institutions of higher learning in developing countries have, over the decades, been churning out tens of thousands of graduates of science who have made no contributions to growth or progress in their countries, other than make a daily living for themselves and their families.

Considering the above, there is a very good case therefore to be made for challenging science students and graduates in universities and technology institutes in developing countries to start coming up with ideas about inventions of new products that will bring about changes in lifestyles in their countries. There is no doubt about it that they face an uphill task financially trying to do this, but this is exactly where their leaders come in – to provide the necessary facilities for research, development and production of prototypes.

Lastly, let us consider the points raised by Mr O'Neil in his article which follows, and particularly the last part of the piece in which he advises on the role of education.

Beyond Nigeria's GDP figures

IN the past year, I have visited Nigeria three times – more than I have travelled to any other country except the United States. I mentioned this to an audience on my most recent trip, saying I wasn't sure what it meant: Am I a leading, coincident or lagging indicator? Maybe I was just there for the power outages – they shield me from the latest news about Manchester United (Don't ask).

Of course, I aspire to be a leading indicator – and I'm hopeful Nigeria and much of the rest of Africa will demonstrate my farsightedness. It's hardly a sure thing, but Nigeria really does have the potential to be a spectacular economic success.

I laid out some reasons for this hope when I nominated the country as one of the "Next 11" emerging economies – countries with lots of people and untapped economic promise, capable of following the path cut by the BRIC nations (Brazil, Russia, India and China). More recently,

I've drawn particular attention to four of the 11, the MINT countries: Mexico, Indonesia, Nigeria and Turkey.

This weekend (April 6), Nigeria rebased its figures for Gross Domestic Product, adding in previously uncounted industries such as telecoms and information technology. On this new basis, the country's GDP was roughly $500 billion in 2013 – making Nigeria's economy the biggest in Africa.

True, even on this new measure, Nigeria accounts for only around 0.5 per cent of global GDP. The whole of Africa has an annual output of only perhaps $2 trillion, comparable to India or Russia. But the region is growing well and its potential is impressive. Nigeria's government has set the goal of becoming one of the world's 20 biggest economies by 2020. I think that's too soon to be likely, but I think Nigeria could be one of the top 15 by 2050.

In this scenario, remembering that Nigeria by then will be home to roughly 20 per cent of Africa's people, the country's growth would power the whole continent. By the middle of this century, Africa's economy would be close to 10 times bigger than it is today. That kind of growth would lift a huge number of Africans out of dire poverty and introduce them to the prosperity that other regions take for granted.

It can be done, but it shouldn't be assumed. African policy makers should be asking whether the recent improvement in the region's economy and the rising interest of foreign investors is thanks to them, or thanks to a decade of strong commodity prices and staggeringly supportive monetary policies in the United States and other advanced economies, causing investors to search far and near for decent returns. The external environment has already turned less friendly. China's growth is slowing, commodity prices have eased, and the US Federal Reserve is scaling back its bond purchases. For Africa, as for other developing economies, this puts the focus back on domestic policy.

Investors, contrary to what you may have heard, distinguish between countries that rise to such challenges and those that don't. The recent strength of financial markets in India and Indonesia reflects, in part, a recognition of those countries' efforts to deal with worsening external imbalances and rising inflation.

After many years of very strong performances, Nigeria's stock markets have been weak lately. This may be nothing more than a correction, but the feud between the government and Lamido Sanusi, former governor of the Central Bank of Nigeria, sure hasn't helped (Sanusi was suspended after he made allegations of mismanagement and misconduct at the state-owned oil company, where billions of dollars in revenues appear to have gone missing. Just this week, a court awarded him damages in a harassment suit he brought against the government).

In the longer term, demography is likely to dominate – along with three other factors: first, the ease with which modern technologies (such as mobile telecoms) can be brought to bear; second, the willingness of ambitious young Africans to travel abroad for education in elite universities in Europe and the United States, then return to seek opportunities at home; and third, the striking energy, ingenuity and creativity that so many Africans – not just the well-travelled – bring to their work.

These things, vital as they may be, need the backing of better governance. Here's a modest suggestion for African ministers, officials and heads of business: Turn up to meetings on time. That kind of thing isn't hard and makes a good impression.

Next, find ways to make economic policy institutions more independent, transparent and honest. This goes double for central banks. Make it a priority to promote trade with neighbouring countries and with the rest of the region, rather than letting old animosities hold this back.

International trade is one of the best ways to succeed, and the continent can easily make big wins here. And finally – maybe most important of all – promote better basic education. A well-educated elite isn't enough.

I do some work for Teach for All, a network of social enterprises that aims to widen educational opportunity. At the recent Nigerian Economic Summit, a Teach for Nigeria initiative was announced. That was good to hear. No nation or region can achieve its potential if its children are denied a decent education. Don't worry too much about commodity prices. They won't decide Africa's future.

O'Neill, former chairman of Goldman Sachs Asset Management, is a Bloomberg View columnist.

CHAPTER NINE

FOOD SUFFICIENCY

It has been decided that this chapter will be the subject of an entirely new book, Food Sufficiency in Developing Countries, which the author will work on, in the few months or years.

The wisdom in importing food [such as rice, palm oil, maize, dates, etc] that can otherwise be grown easily in many developing and third-world countries, will be queried.

The possibility of acquiring large tracts of land for large-scale mechanized agriculture in these countries, construction of farm-houses in them and employment of the hundreds of thousands of unemployed youths in city and town centres in these countries will be considered, the aim, being, for these countries to become self-sufficient and less-dependent on food importation from distant lands, which drains their treasuries.

CHAPTER TEN

THE CLARION CALL

George Orwell once stated that though *Animal Farm* was primarily a satire on the Russian Revolution, he meant the moral to be that revolutions only effect a radical improvement when the masses are alert and know how to chuck out their leaders as soon as the latter have done their job [or failed to]. The turning point of the story was supposed to be when the pigs (amongst the animals in the farm) kept the milk and apple for themselves. A paragraph in Chapter 1 very well and aptly describes the state of affairs in many developing countries today;

But is this simply part of the order of Nature? Is it because this land of ours is so poor that it cannot afford a decent life to those who dwell upon it? No, comrades, a thousand times no! The soil…is fertile, its climate is good, it is capable of affording food in abundance to an enormously greater number of animals [people] than now inhabit it…This single farm [country] of ours would support a dozen horses, twenty cows, hundreds of sheep [millions of people] – and all of them living in a comfort and a dignity that are now almost beyond our imagining. Why then do we continue in this miserable condition? Because nearly the whole of the produce of our labour is stolen from us by human beings [so-called leaders]. There, comrades, is the answer to all our problems.

Then of course followed the rebellion against the farm owners and the animals [people] began to run the farm themselves, in which *'all animals were equal'*, according to the farm's seventh of its seven commandments.

At this point, people of the third world and developing countries are being called upon to take the initiative, remove all non- performing leaders through the democratic process and put in place, administrations that will operate, with set conditions and rules that will ensure that, henceforth, no leaders are ever able to steal or embezzle from the national treasury and that all the resources of their countries are put to judicious use for the over- all benefit of the people.

To achieve, in a global setting, the kind of equality referred to in George Orwell's 'Animal Farm', it must be understood by the leaders and people of third world and developing countries that, in the great gathering of nations today, their contributions do not count for much. Major contributors carry weight, not net contributors. That means that when it comes to crucial matters, their opinions carry no weight whatsoever; therefore no one listens to what they say. Out of courtesy, participants at these conferences from the developed countries listen, often with divided attention, or in a state of slumber, to their statements. The speakers may be eloquent but do not possess the substance – what makes others stop to listen. It is borne out by reports from the general sessions of the United Nations in which the majority of participants walk out when it is the turn of certain speakers from the less-developed countries to talk. On the contrary, the 'main players' are listened to with rapt attention – their remarks are echoed in the press and TV and whatever they say is taken seriously in determining the outcomes of deliberations at such meetings.

Below is a group photograph of world leaders at a recent meeting, with the President of Nigeria [in native attire], alone and virtually neglected! On the next page are comments from readers and followers, about his virtual 'lonely' situation.

David Ologan @davolog 2h
@abati1990 Why is he standing alone looking sad?
Expand

oluseun adetola @sanucrown 2h
@abati1990 GEJ was very afraid
Expand

oluseun adetola @sanucrown 2h
@abati1990 so afraid look at his hand
Expand

Zulkarnaini Abubakar @kwazo03 2h
@abati1990 whts Gej doing their??? He looks harassed
Expand

Just Me @IZEVBIZUAJOHN 2h
@abati1990 is Nigeria a nuclear nation? If NO What is GEJ doing there?
Expand

BENSON ROY @BENSON_ROY 3h
@abati1990 other leaders seem not to know he is also a president he is
looking lost!
Details   ↩ Reply ⇄ Retweet ★ Favorite ⋯ More

Tiny King-Kong™ @LagosLoving 2h
@abati1990 @akinbolaofi fool wearing native attire to a business gathering na
everywhere dem dey do patriotism right clothes 4 diff occasn
Details   ↩ Reply ⇄ Retweet ★ Favorite ⋯ More

Tiny King-Kong™ @LagosLoving 2h
@abati1990 @akinbolaofi he his d one everybody's talking about asking each
other why?
Details   ↩ Reply ⇄ Retweet ★ Favorite ⋯ More

bolaji olayinka @jjgodfather 2h
@abati1990 r u sure this not photoshop? bcos he looked out of place
Details   ↩ Reply ⇄ Retweet ★ Favorite ⋯ More

khidr @hafirofakur 2h
@abati1990 hmm na woo 4 wuna president him no settle his country nd he de
talk of oder country Shame on U
Details   ↩ Reply ⇄ Retweet ★ Favorite ⋯ More

Saheed Bilewu @lanrenikki10 1h
@abati1990 @jimidisu What is he taking away photoshots or potentials?
Details   ↩ Reply ⇄ Retweet ★ Favorite ⋯ More

Bayo Abdulazeez @kssnorgi 1h
@abati1990 what are we doing there?
Details   ↩ Reply ⇄ Retweet ★ Favorite ⋯ More

Richard Ezeife @Brutalistic 1h
@abati1990 perhaps a change of picture is in order Our C-in-C cuts a rather
forlorn and isolated figure
Details   ↩ Reply ⇄ Retweet ★ Favorite ⋯ More

Coco-Bassey Esu @EsuCoco 12h
@abati1990 this picture show how confuse our president on security

In real life and in many western films, people from the third world and developing countries play the much lesser roles of housemaids, gardeners, hospital and office porters and cleaners, bus conductors, cab drivers, railway maintenance crew, etc. That is not to say that some of the people have not risen above these levels – yes, in the medical field, sports, music and business many have carved out a way for themselves, but proportionately, it is only a small percenttage. In spite of this however, the feeling of inequality still appears to suffer from perceived inequalities, for the simple reasons that they are the victims of colonialism and whose home countries have done very little to advance the cause of the human race. They are also fully aware that for these reasons, they and their forebears have been looked down upon for centuries and never really been reckoned with in matters that directly affect the conduct of affairs at global level.

Equality is an abstract term. It is utopian and an ideal. However in order for it to happen, in any human endeavour, there is an implied assumption in the minds of the people about class, target, aspiration, ability and achievement. If we take sprinting as an illustration, if five runners take part in a 100-metres race, usually only one of them will win, or be the fastest. It may not necessarily be the tallest or most strongly built. More than likely it is always down to how much work and preparation the winner has put into it, coupled of course with the fact that he/she has had facilities that were unavailable to the less-lucky runners. How- ever, the fact that he is winner automatically sets him out for awards, prizes, encomium, TV deals, wealth and fame. If one of the other four wants to get to the level where he/she can enjoy the same 'goodies', he/she will have to put their act together, acquire and use the necessary facilities, build up their muscles, train hard, eat the right food, abstain from drugs, alcohol and smoking, etc; this is because, it is apparent that the 'winner' has got something that he/she has not. However, except he is incapacitated in some way, he has within him, the power to change things and this can be done through effort.

We are all witnesses to what the BRICs countries [Brazil, Russia, India and China] have achieved through effort in the last decade. They have all turned around totally dependent and second-rate economies to global powers. India has had a basic commuter car named 'Tata' modelled and built in India for nearly a decade; it has also become a nuclear power and only recently sent a space-ship to Mars. These are no mean achievements but when one considers that this was an exclusive area for a few countries until a decade ago, then it clearly sends out a message to other developing countries that they can do the same. China, whose citizens depended mainly on agriculture until a while back, has now taken the world by storm and become a major manufacturer and exporter – not only that, it has recently commissioned an aircraft carrier! Brazil is building its own ships, locomotives and vehicles Nothing stops other third world and developing countries from taking a cue from these countries, acting alone or together in regional groups, setting themselves targets and achieving what they have achieved.

Now, it needs to be pointed out, for the benefit of all leaders and people of third world and developing countries that there are great benefits to them in actively seeking and pursuing the type of development advanced in the chapter above. First and foremost, their people can become more gainfully employed and their countries conserve much foreign exchange now being wasted on importation of items and luxuries that they can make themselves; these two will invariable translate to progress and development and the good things of life, which is what many of their people hunger after and seek, through migrating.

There are many areas in which a great many ideas can be dreamed up and translated into products and inventions to ease peoples' daily burdens or improve the way things are being done. This is the starting line in the race for third world and develop-ping countries to begin to earn the respect and recognition of those whose ancestors ran the same race decades ago. From the basic items, progress can gradually be made to the bigger machines, for which there are already models or replicas to duplicate. As earlier stated in this work, there is no reason why a country like Nigeria, with proper planning, should not be able to produce its own locally-built [rather than assembled] motor cars within a decade if it wants to. The resources are there both in material and human terms and the skill is not lacking. It just needs a spark from the authorities for research and production centres to be set up and the rest, as the saying goes, can become history.

It is high time that leaders and people of the third world and developing countries began to get their priorities right. There has been so much ground lost in the race that in order to get close [not catch-up] and earn respect, recognition and true equality in the committee of nations, they must begin to make tangible contributions, not just raw materials. It is certainly not right or respectable or proper that one group of people should create the means to make possible the construction of my house, my car, my means of air, sea and road travel, my machines, my personal computer, etc without any input from me whatsoever. It should become a moral issue.

Another way to look at things is, suppose these things have not been made by others? How would we move from our countries to others thousands of miles away? In what types of homes would we live? How will our food be produced and cooked? How would we communicate with our kit and kin thousands of miles away? How would we make our presence felt in this world? How would other people take us seriously and give us the respect we ask of them? Lastly, what shall we tell our children when they ask us what contributions we have made to human development?

AKNOWLEDGEMENT & REFERENCES

1. Statistics and International Development 2002-09

2. ECGD Debt Relief for African countries 2006-07

3. New Statesman

4. Aid & Development – Transparency International

5. Top 10 Investors – T. Pettinger, Oxford, 9/2012

6. O'Neil[Goldman] – Beyond Nigeria's GDP figures

www.ingramcontent.com/pod-product-compliance
Lightning Source LLC
Chambersburg PA
CBHW060150300526
45790CB00014B/481